Relationships

Bond or Bondage

2 BOOKS IN 1

Relationships

Bond or Bondage

2 BOOKS IN 1

SADHGURU

JAICO PUBLISHING HOUSE

Ahmedabad Bangalore Bhopal Chennai
Delhi Hyderabad Kolkata Lucknow Mumbai

Published by Jaico Publishing House
A-2 Jash Chambers, 7-A Sir Phirozshah Mehta Road
Fort, Mumbai - 400 001
jaicopub@jaicobooks.com
www.jaicobooks.com

To be sold only in India, Bangladesh, Bhutan,
Pakistan, Nepal, Sri Lanka and the Maldives.

RELATIONSHIPS: BOND OR BONDAGE
ISBN 978-93-86867-50-6

First Jaico Impression: 2018
20th Jaico Impression: 2020

Page design and layout: Inosoft Systems, Delhi

Printed by
Snehesh Printers, Mumbai

Contents

Introduction

Human beings constantly make and break relationships. Unfortunately, relationships can make and break human beings too. No one cherishes slavery, but many of us have enslaved ourselves to our relationships. As the relationship goes through its highs and lows, we get caught in the wake, and bounce back and forth between happiness and dejection. And sadly, the lows seem to come too often and the highs seem to pass too soon.

Despite this, human beings yearn for relationships. Even a broken heart – scarred by love lost – pursues and rejoices in love again. But as time marches past, the euphoria of the new is cast aside by the tedium of the old. The very relationships we once coveted, suffocate us and we seek escape. Lovers quarrel, parents and children grow weary of each other, and friendships run out of steam. So the old is discarded, but then once again the quest for the new begins afresh. Relationships! We can't live with them, we can't live without them.

Why are relationships such a circus for most of us? What is this primal urge within us that demands a bond – physical, mental, or emotional – with another? And how do we keep this bond from turning into bondage? The answer lies in the basis upon which we build our relationships. Do we form and maintain relationships to fulfill our needs, or do we do it to express our joy? Are we extracting something or are we sharing something? These are the fundamental questions that this book looks at.

Sadhguru shares with us the keys to forming lasting and joyful bonds, whether they are with husband or wife, family and friends, at work, or with the very existence itself. Logical beyond debate, yet speaking in a blend of unconditional love and blatant honesty that only a Guru can express, Sadhguru looks at why people build expectations around their relationships, and how we can turn these expectations around, to create a beautiful bond.

As the book unfolds, he answers questions on why we come together in the first place, and examines the various levels on which human beings create relationships – the physical body, the mind, the emotional scape, and the life energies. He reveals that the only relationship that can last beyond life and death is one made on the level of the life energies. "There is a dimension of relationship which is not of the body, which is not of physicality, which is not of companionship or emotional proximity, but simply of basic life energy," he tells us. Exploring the possibility of living an absolutely fulfilling and complete life without the need for any kind of relationship at all, Sadhguru tells us that to live magically, without emotional inadequacies or ungratified physical compulsions, is within the reach of every human being, if only we make the journey from compulsiveness to consciousness.

Isha Publications

"Don't try to manage the other person. Just see how to include the other person."

Human relationships are a funny thing. If you look at any relationship that human beings hold with each other, it means a lot to people – most people could not live without it – but at the same time, most relationships bring more pain than joy, more entanglement than freedom, more acrimony than love. It is for a few moments of rapport and oneness which people share, that they are willing to sacrifice their whole life. Those few moments are so precious to them.

Relationships are of so many different kinds. The first relationship that all of us hold, starts with the mother – the comfort of the womb, the nourishment of the bosom, the tenderness of care and other things that come with it. The next relationship is maybe with the father – of support, security, and guidance. Then come teachers and friends, a relationship of learning and sharing. Then come spouses, lovers, children, and other kinds of associations and relationships in the social structure.

Everything has something to give and everything has something to take. It is only because a certain emotional need is, to some extent, fulfilled by these relationships that one can continue with them. Those people who logically examine their relationships can never stay in any relationship. If you logically look, "Is it really worthwhile?" then nothing will stand the test of your logic. Somewhere, there is a certain kind of fulfillment. There have been moments of joy, sharing, oneness, and of course, moments of support, and security; but more than anything, there is the fear of being alone.

It is not necessarily always love which brings relationships. The fear of being alone is the major reason why people stay together, not only in marriage but in everything else. Yet, still, because there are moments of emotional fulfillment, people hang on. This is not with any one type of relationship, but with just about every kind of relationship that human beings can hold.

On a certain day, a husband and wife were driving after a serious argument and disagreement. The problem with the car is you cannot get up and leave. If it is a home situation, before it picks up too much heat, they get up and move into some other space – the space saves them. But in the car, the damn thing is locked and you are going at a certain speed, so you cannot get off. If you get off, it could be for good! So after an argument and some nasty moments, this husband and wife were giving each other the silent treatment. Then, they were passing by a farm where there were a few mules, pigs, and goats. The husband saw the wife was paying lots of attention to those animals. "Must be relatives, hmm?"

She said, "Yeah. In-laws."

These things are not happening between people who hate each other. These things happen between people who love each other. This is all a love affair. If they hated each other, they would do something else really nasty which would end things. The problem is they love each other, but this is how it finds expression because they can express their meanness to each other only within the legal limits!

A woman went shopping and when she came to the counter to pay, she opened a bag and as usual, whatever she needed was always at the bottommost part of the bag. So she pulled out everything and also happened to keep the television remote outside while searching for her wallet.

The salesperson looked at this and asked, "Do you always carry your television remote with you?"

She said, "No, I asked my husband to come shopping with me, and this is the meanest thing I can do legally."

If you break the television it becomes illegal. The meanest thing that you can do is, you can take away the remote and put it back later.

You as a person are a body, a certain accumulation of experience and information which has formed certain attitudes. A certain kind of mind, a certain kind of body, a certain type of emotion, certain types of likes and dislikes, certain types of opinions – a bundle of all this is "you." The same ingredients but of a different kind is "the other" in the relationship. They are the same ingredients, but the two do not fit. There are moments when suddenly, it seems to fit and everything is beautiful, everything – the physicality, the mentality, the emotional aspect – is compatible. But the next moment, whichever way you try, it does not fit.

This is all two people are trying to do in every relationship, whether they are friends, parents, spouses or something else. A body, a mind and an emotional setup are trying to somehow fit into another body, another mind, and another emotional setup. These two bodies, minds, and emotions can never, ever fit perfectly every moment of twenty-four hours. It is not just *you* who has a problem with someone that it is not fitting. Every body is unique, every mind is unique, every set of emotions is unique. They can never fit into another one perfectly. If anyone thinks there is such a possibility, he is going to waste his life. If he understands that it is only at certain moments when it can fall into place, otherwise it cannot, then he will conduct it in a certain way.

People are trying to create relationships based on too much fantasy; it is not rooted in reality. A fantasy can be in a good state today, but can be a bad trip tomorrow. Instead of trying to manage our relationships – which is truly impossible actually – if you just learn to include the other as a part of yourself, your life becomes an expression of joyfulness not a pursuit of happiness. Then you will see, relationships have various colors, but every color and hue that it takes on could be enjoyed. In this inclusion, all the differences are okay. But if you try to manage relationships with your brilliant management, it will just give you hell. The smartest people on the planet – or those people who think they are really smart – tend to have the most horrible relationships. Not essentially, but generally. People who are just simple have wonderful relationships because it is not the question of management.

Nobody likes to be "managed." When they realize you are managing them, they will give you hell. They will make your life miserable in so many ways. For most people on this planet, it is not their enemies who are taking their life; it is their loved ones. If your enemy is taking your life, there is some sense to it, but people who care for each other are the ones who are taking each other's lives. This is happening constantly. Generation after generation, people are going through the same things because they believe the other person has to be managed. Don't try to manage the other person. Just see how to include them. Then, even if you don't understand what the hell is happening with them, it is still okay.

You need a relationship only because somewhere, there is some sense of incompleteness in you. If you take away this, if you attain to that state within you which has nothing to do with the other, then every other person wants to be with you. Everyone wants to be with you because your need is gone. This is the funny thing about life – when you have a need, nobody wants to be with you. When your need is gone, everyone wants to be with you. It is only when the flower blossoms the bees will come; if you don't blossom bees won't come. If you are a closed bud and you call the bees, they won't come. If you open up, you don't have to call; they will anyway come.

So if you want to have wonderful relationships, do not try to manage the relationship. See how to enhance who you are on all levels – physically, mentally, emotionally, and energy-wise.

If you enhance yourself into a very beautiful state, everyone will want to hold a relationship with you. If you do not enhance yourself and try to manage everything, it is going to be very stressful. A human being should always focus on how to enhance his way of being. Then, everything else gets naturally managed. Whether it is your profession, your relationship or whatever else in your life, it will happen to its best only when who you are is enhanced.

1

Within Four Walls

❧

"You could simply be loving with just about anything, and that is how you should be with the whole existence."

Questioner: *Nowadays, for many reasons, relationships of love and marriage have turned into misery. Could you go a little deeper and speak about love and marriage?*

Sadhguru: The only reason marriages have become miserable is because two people have lost their ability to laugh at themselves and joke about each other. They become dead serious about a simple arrangement made by two people to make each other's life. It is a simple arrangement that you are making because two people have needs and want to live together. But you become so dead serious about it that it becomes a miserable arrangement. This is not because there is something wrong with marriage. It is only because you cannot joke or laugh that everything becomes a dead serious issue. People will go out with their friends and laugh and joke about the same issues, but when they come home, all these become serious issues. Do you see this happening? It becomes a miserable process if you do that.

So what is love? If you have to understand and above all if you have to make it work, it is best you understand the engineering and mechanics of love. Love happens to you only when you are willing to respond.

It happened once that Shankaran Pillai was at the university. One day he went to his professor and said, "Professor, I need your help."

The professor said, "Sure, that's why I'm here. Please tell me, what can I do?"

Shankaran Pillai named the college beauty and said, "I am in love with her, and I am fifty percent successful, but I need your help."

The professor said, "Well this is not an area where I am authorized to help you. If it is anything academic I can help you, but anyway you asked me – so what do you mean by fifty percent successful?"

Shankaran Pillai said, "I am completely in love with her, but she is not aware of it. One fifty percent is handled. You must help me with the other fifty percent."

Love is just your ability to respond to someone. The moment I say "love," you think of someone. Love is not about someone. Love is about you. You can walk on the street lovingly, you can work in your office lovingly.

Sometime ago, we were doing a program for the top forty executives of Microsoft. I had about eleven volunteers around me. Our volunteers were all fully fired up, all the time on, doing things. These executives are constantly looking for good people to work with, because that is the main challenge. Getting the right kind of people to be around you is eighty percent of your work. If you have the right kind of people around you, the rest is simple. So they looked around and then they asked, "Sadhguru, where do you get these people?"

I said, "You don't get them, you have to make them."

"How do you make them?"

I said, "You have to make them fall in love with you."

"How do we do that?"

I said, "First you have to fall in love with them."

Love is not something that you do. Love is the very way you are. It is your quality. If you make this your quality, then relationships will happen according to different types of needs that you have. Today, unfortunately, if you say "relationship" in the West, people will immediately think of a body-based relationship with a man or woman. In India if you say "relationship," we think mother, father, brother, sister, friend, all kinds. But now, even in India, all the urban, westernized youth think relationship means body-based, sex-based relationships. It is very unfortunate.

You are particularly talking about body-based relationships, where maximum intimacy and conflict happens. For most, not always, but for most married couples, if they do not have children within five to six years of getting married, their relationship will fall apart or at least become meaningless. They have become half-dead to each other. There are some people who can keep it up for their lifetime, that is different, but for lots of them their relationship will fall apart.

When a child arrives, with this bundle of joy, unknowingly you laugh, you sing, you crawl under the sofa behind the child, you do all kinds of things that you would have never done otherwise. Your life comes back to you once again. But when the child grows up and is trying to find his own life, and he does something that you do not like, immediately you say, "You know how much I have done for you?" No – you got back your life only because of your child. But now you are claiming, "How much I have done for you!" It is a completely wrong approach.

This is happening in every relationship. Instead of recognizing that someone is fulfilling your needs, you think you are doing a great job for them. When something goes wrong somewhere, you think, "He is responsible." The moment you point your finger towards someone, this is the beginning of a bad relationship.

Relationships are about people. Different relationships need to be conducted in different ways. But love is not about someone. It is not relation-specific. You could simply be loving with just about anything, and that is how you should be with the whole existence. Because this is not about the existence; this is about the way *you* exist. You exist in a loving manner and build relationships according to needs. You cannot behave the same way with every individual just because you love everyone. How you behave and conduct your relationship with a particular person depends on the level of intimacy with that person. That is the judiciousness you have to develop; there is no readymade solution for that. But if you are loving, your life experience has become extremely pleasant. How someone else is does not matter because you feel absolutely pleasant and wonderful within yourself. That is important.

If you feel wonderful within, you will naturally do wonderful things to other people. If you feel nasty within, you will naturally share your nastiness with other people. In that sense, love is a very important factor in everyone's life. Love means your emotions have become pleasant. If your emotions are pleasant, you are naturally loving. Whatever you look upon, you will look upon them lovingly – whether it is a man, woman, child, tree, animal, bird, or just the air that you breathe. Can't you inhale the air you breathe lovingly? Air has memory. If the air remembers, "This person loves me," it will behave wonderfully. Can't you drink water lovingly? Water has memory. This is a scientific fact. If water remembers that it is being consumed lovingly, it will go and do wonderful things to you. Otherwise it will go and do nasty things to you.

Try this – the food that you eat, the air that you breathe, the water that you drink, the earth that you walk upon, just approach it all lovingly. Just see how your life will change! Everything about you will change dramatically, including your health situation. You touch everything lovingly because everything has memory. Isn't this true with human beings? During some little situation even with a total stranger on the street, if you approach that person lovingly, even if you were to meet this person two years later in some other situation, won't he respond to you in a certain way? So love is not relation-specific. Love is your quality. You can touch everything lovingly. Above all, your way of being becomes utterly pleasant and beautiful, which is most important.

"'Man and woman' are two compulsions. Two compulsions can never live together."

Questioner: *Why is it that love and marriage often create the maximum conflict between people?*

Sadhguru: "Man" and "woman" are physically, kind of opposite. Nature has made us this way so that the process of reproduction happens and the next generation becomes a possibility. If that was not necessary – if storks were dropping babies from the skies – we would not need a man and a woman to work for the future generations to come. And if there wasn't a deep sense of compulsion about the reproductive process, people would not go for it. Every cell in your body, including your brain cells, are taken over by hormones and compel and propel you in that direction. It takes enormous intelligence for a person to rise beyond that. Otherwise it looks like this *is* life – it makes you feel like that. Till you were ten or eleven years old, you did not even think about it. Whatever the other people were doing looked funny. But suddenly, this new chemical took over the body and now it is all an absolute reality.

You have been drugged and chemically sabotaged by nature to fulfill its own purpose of reproduction, continuation, and perpetuation of the species. Once this happened, now somehow, man and woman are compelled to come together. Or in other words, once this compulsion comes, naturally the mind begins to work in that way as to how to get the best out of it.

Fundamentally, a relationship is unfortunately happening with an intention to somehow make use of each other. It is a give-and-take relationship. When you are giving and taking on a daily basis, always one person will feel, "I am giving more, the other person is giving less."

Societies have always taught you that to be smart is to give less and take more. Whether it is a marketplace or a marriage, it is the same calculation. This is why there is so much talk about love, so that you transcend this calculation. When you are emotionally overwhelmed by someone, you transcend the calculation. It becomes, "What I take is not important; what I give is important." The relationship runs beautifully when it is at that level of emotional intensity. Once that emotional intensity drops, it just becomes give-and-take. You do give-and-take in your business, with your neighbor, with so many people, but those transactions are limited – the give-and-take in a marriage is constant, and you are caged with this particular person constantly. So naturally you feel that in some way, you are being used by someone else. Once this comes in, there is conflict, conflict, conflict.

Only in moments of love, can a man and woman really be together. Once that is not there, it is very difficult. The physicality and emotionality of it and other aspects of sharing and living become a struggle. Especially because the physical body is involved, they can very easily feel that they are being used by someone. If it was just money, if it was just a house, there is some settlement, "Okay, you use that part of the house, I will use this part of the house." "You cook, I will earn." But because the body is involved, very easily one will feel used, so there is conflict.

Questioner: *So what is the solution?*

Sadhguru: You should stop being a man or woman all the time. You don't have to carry your manhood or womanhood twenty-four hours of the day. There are certain situations in certain aspects of life where you need to be a man or a woman. The rest of the time, you do not have to be either. But societies have trained you to be like this all the time. From the very clothes that you wear and the way you do everything – you have been trained in a certain way, to serve a certain purpose. Once you become like this – twenty-four hours man or twenty-four hours woman – you are troubled. But if you know how to simply be a piece of life, you will be fine, and when there is a requirement that you have to be a man or woman, you can play your role pretty well. So please save it. Don't just go on spreading it around in the street. Just walk and live as a piece of life. Only in a certain situation you have to be a man or a woman; you can be a wonderful human being at that time. If you are like this, there will be no conflict. It will be just fine. Two human beings can live together.

"Man and woman" are two compulsions. Two compulsions can never live together. The more identified you are with your sexuality, the more compulsive you will become. When you are compulsive, naturally you will step over many people. Once you start stepping on each other, there will be trouble. If you do not identify yourself too much with your womanhood or manhood and if you just walk as a piece of life, you will see that it is such a minor part of your life. You do not have to structure your life around it.

So much of your potential would find expression if you just do not get too identified with your sexuality. People would become so much more creative and so much more capable of various things that they have not imagined.

"Love is just a currency for blissfulness."

Questioner: *Love seems to be the driving force in my life. I think I am a little confused about being one with someone versus having unconditional love for someone.*

Sadhguru: Is it really unconditional?

Questioner: *I don't know. Okay, maybe not.*

Sadhguru: There are any number of conditions, isn't it? All the conditions you have set for the other person, all the expectations you have of the other person – if they are all broken tomorrow morning, the same love will turn into anger and then into hatred. So if we have to maintain your love, we have to control the other person in such a way that he does only what you expect him to do! Otherwise, this wonderful love will turn into very nasty anger.

I am not trying to belittle relationships. But there is nothing wrong in looking at the limitations of what it is. That is how limited it is, but that does not mean it has no beauty. Suppose you look at a flower. The flower is so beautiful, but if I just crush it, it will become pieces, and then become manure in two days. I can destroy this flower in a moment, but does that reduce the beauty and significance of what the flower is? No. Similarly, your love is fragile. Don't believe fanciful things about it. At the same time, I am not denying the beauty that is attached to it.

Still, when you make such a fragile dimension of life the foundation of your life, naturally you will be anxiety-ridden all the time because you are sitting on such a fragile flower. Suppose you built your house not on the earth but on a flower because it is beautiful; you will always live in fear. If you built your foundations on the earth and looked at the flower, smelt it and touched it, that would be wonderful. But if you built your house *on* the flower, you are constantly in fear. I am speaking only in that context. We are not trying to deny what love is.

On one level if you look at it – I do not want to generalize this totally, but for many people it is so – love is just one more need without which they cannot live. As the body has its needs, the emotion has its needs. When I say, "I cannot live without you," it is not any different from me saying, "I cannot walk without a crutch." If you had a diamond-encrusted crutch, you could very easily fall in love with it. And if after you used this crutch for ten years, I tell you, "Now you can walk free," you say "No, how can I leave my crutch?" – there is no life sense in it.

This is the same thing. In the name of love, you make yourself so absolutely helpless and incomplete within yourself. Does it mean to say there is no beauty and no other dimension to this? There is. There have been many people who lived in such a way that they could not exist without the other. If it really becomes like that, that two beings have become like one, that is wonderful.

This happened to a king in India. He was in Rajasthan. He had a young wife who loved him and was totally dedicated to him. But kings always had a whole range of concubines. So he thought it was quite silly, the way she was deeply engrossed in him. He was amused and he liked the attention, but sometimes it was too much. Then he would shake her off a little bit, and carry on with many others, but the woman was totally dedicated to him.

The king and queen had two talking mynas, which are tropical birds that can speak better than parrots if you train them. One day, one of these birds died, and the other one just sat there without eating food. The king did everything possible to feed the bird, but the bird just would not take in any food and died in two days' time.

This somehow touched the king. "What is this? It is natural for any life to value its own life first. But this bird just sat there and died."

When he said this, the wife said, "When someone really loves someone else, it is very natural for them to go away with the other, because life would not mean anything for them later."

The king jokingly asked, "Is that so for you? Do you love me that much?"

She said, "Yes, it is so for me." The king was very amused by this.

One day, the king went out hunting with his friends. This thought about the birds dying and his wife saying that it was also true for her was sort of playing in his mind. He really wanted to check it out. So he took his clothes, bloodied them and sent them back to the palace with someone who announced, "The king was mauled by a tiger and killed." The queen received his clothes with great dignity, without a tear in her eyes. She arranged for firewood, put the clothes on top of it, and then laid herself on the firewood and died. People just could not believe this. The queen just lay down and left. There was nothing else to do because she was dead, so they cremated her. When the news went to the king, he was broken. Just on a whim he wanted to play with her and she actually died – not committing suicide – she left just like that.

People have loved like this because somewhere, two beings got entwined. In India, marriage was always conducted like this traditionally. There was a whole science behind it which has become a joke today. When two people were to be married, the compatibility of not just the families and bodies was looked at. They looked at a deeper compatibility – a certain energy compatibility was looked at and the marriage was fixed. Most of the time, the two people would not have even seen each other.

It did not matter because the compatibility had been fixed by someone who knew this better than them. But if they themselves make choices, they would make choices depending upon the shape of the nose, the eyes and this and that – which will not mean anything three days after the wedding. If your wife has wonderful eyes but she only glares at you, what is the point?

When marriages were fixed by someone who knew, they prepared something, which we extensively use today in yoga, called a *mangalsutra*. Mangalsutra means a sacred thread. Preparing a sacred thread is an elaborate science. We make a few strands of raw cotton, smear it with vermilion and turmeric, and then it is energized in a certain way. Once this is tied, it is for life and beyond. There have been experiments where the same couples have remained as couples for lifetimes, consciously choosing to be like that because they employed ways to tie people together not just on the physical or emotional level. What you do on the level of the body, mind and emotion goes with death. But what you do on the level of the energy stays on. You actually tie peoples' *nadis*[1] together, and this is why it was considered that once it is done, it is for life. There is no question of reconsidering because something far deeper than your understanding has been tied together by people who knew what to do. Nowadays, the same procedure is done but by people who do not know what to do. So naturally people are refusing, "We don't want to wear the damn thread." Whether you wear it or not does not mean anything now, because the science behind it has been lost.

When it was done by someone who knew how to do it, then for those two people, it does not arise in their mind, "Should this person be my wife or not?" "Is this man going to be my

---

[1] Channels through which the life force or *prana* flows in the energy body.

husband forever?" It just goes on. Even with death it does not stop. There are any number of couples in India where if one dies, within a few months the other one will follow even if they are healthy, simply because the energies were tied like this. If you are bound like that with another human being, that two beings exist as one, that is a wonderful way to exist. It is not an ultimate possibility, but still it is a beautiful way to live.

Today, when people talk about love, they are talking only about the emotional part of it. Emotions will say one thing today and another thing tomorrow. When you first made the relationship you thought, "This is forever," but within three months you think, "Oh, why the hell am I with this person?" Because it is all going by what you like and what you do not like. In this kind of relationship, you will only suffer, because when a relationship is unstable and is broken off and on like this, you will go through enormous pain and suffering which is totally unnecessary.

The idea of love is not to create pain, though a lot of poetry about pain has been written. The reason why you go into love is because it is supposed to bring you blissfulness. Love is not the goal; blissfulness is the goal. People are mad about falling in love with someone, though they have been wounded and bruised any number of times, because when they thought they were in love, there was a little bit of blissfulness in them. Love is just a currency for blissfulness. Right now, that is the only way most people know how to be blissful.

But there is a way to be blissful irrespective of this way or that way. If you are blissful, then being loving is not a problem – anyway you will be. Only when you are seeking blissfulness through love, then you are very selective about whom to be loving with. But when you are blissful, whatever you see, you can be loving with that, what is the problem? Because there is no fear of entanglement. When there is no fear of entanglement, only then you will know involvement with life.

"If you go on playing around with too many people, after sometime you become numb."

Questioner: *Sadhguru, is being loving different from falling in love with someone? I find that I keep looking for a new relationship every so often because the old one doesn't really work out.*

Sadhguru: If you do this exercise of falling in love too often, after sometime you will not like anyone in the world. Charles Lamb was a famous English essayist. On a certain day, someone came and told Charles Lamb that he wanted to introduce someone to him. Charles Lamb said, "No, I don't want to meet him. I don't like the man." He said, "You don't like the man! You have not even met him. How can you say you don't like him?" Charles Lamb said, "That's why I don't like him. I have not met him."

If you go on playing around with too many people, after sometime you become numb. You don't like anyone because there is something called as *runanubandha*.

Runanubandha is a certain aspect of *karma*; it is a certain structure of *karmic* substance. Wherever a certain amount of meeting and mingling happens between people, some runanubandha is created. Especially when two bodies come together, the runanubandha is much deeper. It is a kind of recording in the body; the body is keeping a record of everything that has happened. If intimacy happened with another body, it is keeping a record of that particular kind of energy.

Because the body remembers. If there are multiple partners, the body slowly gets confused over a period of time and this confusion will tell in your life in a million different ways. Your mind is confused, but you are living with that somehow. If the body gets confused, then you are in deep trouble.

In many ways, one of the major reasons for the level of anxiety, the level of insecurity, and the level of depression that is going on right now is just that the bodies are confused. After sometime, you do not need any reason to go nuts. People are just going nuts without any reason because the body itself is confused.

The body will get confused with multiple intimacies, that is one thing. Another thing is the type of food that you eat. Whenever a little affluence comes, people think they have to eat everything in a single meal. In India, orthodox people never ate more than two or three items in a meal, and those three items were always matched together; they were not mismatched food. People understood the body so well that in our homes, they knew that when they cook a particular vegetable, they will make only a particular kind of curry. When they cook this vegetable, another kind will never be made because traditionally, we understood that if we put this and that together, the body gets confused. Once your body gets confused you will go haywire in so many ways. This understanding was always there.

These are two major things – people not eating properly and an indiscriminate sense of intimacy with other bodies – which will create a certain confusion on the body level which will take a toll over a period of time. "Have I committed a sin? Is this a punishment for me?" It is not on that level. Every action has a consequence. This is not a moralistic reality; it is a certain existential process. If you do certain things with your mind, certain consequences will come. If you do certain things with your body, certain consequences will come.

These are things that have been deeply understood and life was structured in a certain way around that. Now, in the name of freedom we want to demolish everything and suffer. Maybe centuries later we will realize that this is not the way to live.

⌇

"You can use everything for your growth, if that is all your focus is."

Questioner: *Sadhguru, if you are in a very unsupportive relationship with someone, how can you move ahead on the spiritual path without getting stuck?*

Sadhguru: If your concern is spiritual growth, then if you have a demon for your partner, that is the best thing! But your husband or your wife is not just about spiritual growth. If you also want to have a pleasant life in the family, you have to choose someone whom you like. But there is always something that you do not like about any human being on the planet, isn't it? You use that part of it for your spiritual growth, and the rest of it you enjoy, as life.

If your intention is to have a good family, then some rapport is needed between two people. Otherwise it will not work. Especially if you have children, then rapport is a must. Otherwise, you will foul up the new life that has come. Nobody has any right to do that, but people are doing it. You can mess yourself up as much as you want, that is up to you. But you cannot mess a fresh life that is just coming up. That is not taken seriously because reproduction happens so easily. I wish reproduction was a more difficult enterprise. Then, only those who really want to would have gone for it. It is such an easy and compulsive enterprise that it simply happens.

If you are looking for a good family life, then one has to find rapport, and that rapport means that there are some areas of commonality at least. If you are looking for a spiritual life, it does not matter what kind of person he or she is. You can use everything for your growth, if that is all your focus is. But generally your focus is both ways – you want to have a little bit of that and a little bit of this. It is a mixed fare, so it gets a little complex.

To build a rapport takes effort, it takes compromise, it takes love and it takes endurance. If you want to build a rapport with someone who is not supportive, but you do not want to go his way, it takes lots of endurance. People whom you love are not easy.

So what can you do? One thing is to transform yourself in such a way, that being in your presence, unknowingly, they will turn around.

Sometime ago, I went out and it started raining. I was carrying both my phones because I was expecting some calls. One phone is for India, and one is for outside-India calls. I had one in my jacket and the other in my trouser pocket, and they got wet and both the phones got fried. Then people around me were telling me, "Sadhguru, why carry two phones? Now, we can have two SIM cards in one phone. This is a Chinese phone. If you hold it one way, you can speak on the India SIM card. If you turn it around, it just shifts into the other SIM card. You don't have to switch anything." I did not get the phone, but you must become like this if you wish to take people who are around you with you. If you want to walk alone, it is very easy. If you want to take people with you, then it takes a considerable amount of effort.

Gautama was asked this question, "Is it better to walk alone on the path or with a companion?"

He said, "It is better to walk alone than to walk with a fool."

Because they can take such a lot of energy and time, and you do not know, they may be stronger than you and take you their way rather than you taking them your way. There is every possibility.

I will not say what Gautama said. All I am saying is, it does not matter how you walk – as far as your spiritual process is concerned, anyway you are alone. Nobody is with you. It is only the bodily process, the material process of life, which you can share with people. You come alone and you go alone. Even if you have a twin brother or sister, you still come alone and go alone. When it comes to the spirit, anyway you walk alone. Do not mix that up. That part of it you handle well. The material part of it, handle it according to your capability. You must see what you are capable of and what you are not capable of. If your partner comes your way, it is wonderful. If they do not, it is alright. Do not grudge them. It is just that you do not have to go that way.

Different people need different kinds of impetus. If they are sensible, they learn by just looking. If they are not sensible, they learn by a thrashing. Life will thrash them. You make sure you handle the spiritual part of your life hundred percent properly. The material part of your life is never hundred percent proper, and it never can be. Is there any family which is a perfect family? Is there any business which is a perfect business? There is no such thing. Don't seek that. Your life will become wasteful and fanciful if you seek such things. They all happen to the extent you are capable of handling them.

"Whoever is next to you right now, if you give yourself totally, if you show total involvement, you will see, just anyone is fine."

Questioner: *My mother always feels that I have not chosen the right partner for my life. She feels that my wife is not the best. Why is it that mothers-in-law and daughters-in-law do not get along which each other?*

Sadhguru: This is a fundamental problem in most human beings: they are always looking for the best person or the best thing to do in their life. There is no best person nor is there a best thing to do on this planet. Whatever you do, if you put your heart into it and really throw yourself, it becomes a great thing to do. Whoever is next to you right now, if you give yourself totally and show total involvement, you will see just anyone is fine. If you think, "Is this the best person?" nobody in the world is the best person. Even if you get married to God, you will still complain. Not just your mother – you yourself will complain.

When you say "a mother," essentially she is a woman. Then she became a mother. When you say "a wife," essentially she is a woman, then she became a wife. It is a secondary role. Her basic identity is that of being a woman. The next identity is maybe a wife, and then a mother.

It once happened in the state of Ohio in the USA. A young man decided to get married. The boy told his mother he was getting married, and that he wanted to bring the girl home. It is not a question of approval, but still, a question of blessing and a little bit of approval so that "cats and dogs" kind of things do not happen in the house.

He was very fond of his mother, so he wanted to make it a little challenging and humorous for her.

He brought three young women who were office colleagues of his, along with his girlfriend. They all came for dinner and the mother was supposed to find out who the intended girl is. He behaved very close with all of them so that she would not figure it out. After they had all left, he asked, "Mama, do you know which is my girl?"

She said, "The one who was wearing the red vest."

He said, "How did you know? I didn't even look at her. I was always glancing at the others just so that you don't know."

She said, "The moment she walked in, I didn't like her. So it had to be her."

There is an instinctive rejection or instinctive resistance to the new woman who is coming into the house, because you are now required to share someone who belonged to you with someone else in an unequal proportion – not even in equal proportion. Somewhere as a mother, she wants her son to get married, she wants him to have a wife, she wants him to be happy – all that is true. But on another level, she is still a woman. She has to now seek permission to share something that belonged to her. That makes things a little difficult. Unfortunately, the same stupid relationship problems have been going on for centuries endlessly. It could be changed, but people have not decided to change it.

Questioner: *You make it sound almost biological.*

Sadhguru: It is somewhat biological because it is all a process of procreation and protection. If a woman is not possessive about what belongs to her, she would not have taken care of her baby. She would have just delivered it, left it and walked away. If you look at an animal, let us say an elephant, once it delivers, for three days it does not allow anyone to come there because it is so possessive of what belongs to it. The tusker which impregnated the elephant has gone. He does not care about the calf that was born. But a woman is possessive. If a woman was not possessive, the early part of childhood would not happen for any child. So it is biological and that extends itself throughout life in some way or the other. Generally, a lot of women do not grow out of it, but if one is mature and aware, one can grow out of it.

"When a child enters your house, it is not time to become a teacher; it is time to learn."

Questioner: *What does being a good parent mean? What does it really involve when it comes to children?*

Sadhguru: Somehow, most adults assume that as soon as a child is born, it is time to become teachers. When a child enters your house, it is not time to become a teacher; it is time to learn. If you look at yourself and your child, who is more joyous? Your child, isn't it? It is time you learn life from him, not the other way around. The only thing that you can teach your child – which you have to, to some extent – is a few survival tricks: how to survive and make a few bucks in the world. But when it comes to life itself, a child knows more about life experientially, by himself. He is life; he knows it. Even with you, if you take away the influences you have imposed upon your mind, your life energies know how to *be*. It is only your mind which does not know how to be. All that you are going to impose upon your child is your mind, which is already confused, miserable, and so many things. I am not saying everyone is miserable that way, but you are capable of all kinds of imagined sufferings. Your child has still not gone there.

It is time to learn, not teach. The only thing that you can give is an atmosphere of love, care and support for the child to grow. Good parenting is not about teaching the child what to do and what not to do; it is about creating an atmosphere. If you want to grow your garden, you don't sit there every day and try to extract flowers or fruits out of it. You simply maintain the atmosphere and the child grows well. That is all you can do, and that is all that should be done.

It is because most parents are looking at their children as an extension of themselves that they want their children to be like them. Otherwise they feel lost and insecure. They even start wondering where their children came from because they are so unlike them. Your children need not be like you. The next generation of people should not think and feel like you. They should think and feel and do things that you never even dared to think of. One of the main reasons why parents are constantly trying to teach what they know to the child is because there is a need in them to extend themselves through their children. Or in other words, they are trying to squeeze life out of their children to make their own life. It is not necessary. This need has come because of a sense of incompleteness and insecurity about life. If this is dropped, they will know what to do with the child.

If parents are truly concerned about their children, they must raise them in such a way that they will never have any need for the parent. The process of loving should always be a liberating process, not an entangling process. But in so many ways, parents are trying to entangle the child as theirs, because after a certain age, your identity is entirely through the children. Initially, your identities are in other ways, but once your children come to a certain stage, you are trying to identify yourself through your children. You are trying to live through them, so you want them to be somehow conducive to your way of being and thinking and feeling. It need not be so at all. They can be something absolutely different from you.

If you experience the being you *are* as a complete being, then the need to make your life through someone else or to extract life through someone else does not arise. A child is in many ways the most helpless and the most exploited on the planet because he has no defenses against you. "No, I am not doing anything wrong. I don't beat him or abuse him." That is not the point – you are imposing your thoughts and your emotions upon him. He is totally defenseless against this.

When the child is born, allow the child to look around, spend time with nature and with himself. Create an atmosphere of love and support and do not try to impose your morals, ideas, religion or whatever in any way. Allow him to grow, allow his intelligence to grow and help him look at life on his own terms, as a human being – not identified with the family, or your wealth or whatever else. Helping him look at life as a human being is very essential for his wellbeing and the wellbeing of the world.

At the same time, there are other forces in society trying to influence him all the time. The influence of education, of friends, of the street on which your children walk – all this is definitely there. One way or the other we have unconsciously built this social structure and those influences cannot be eliminated 100%. It is just that you can only help and support the child to look at life from his intelligence, not your way or their way. Right now, the influence of the street is strong on the child and you are trying to influence him the other way. He will resist because for so many reasons, street culture is so much more attractive than home culture when you are young.

Most of the time, parents are trying to counter-influence their children, which only pushes them into the street more.

The perils of the street are always there. The perils of the street are the perils of living in this world. It could be drugs, it could be an accident, it could be an injury, it could be death, it could be alcohol, it could be various perversions – all these things are there. But what you need to understand is that whether you like it or not, today or tomorrow, your child has to learn to live with his own intelligence, making his own choices as to how much of what he has to do in his life. The sooner he gets equipped for this, the better. This does not mean you push a young child on the street to learn his own ways or you try to counter-influence him with your own morality and values. You help him look at his life with his own intelligence, rather than be influenced. In many ways, he is probably taking sustenance from the street only because there is a certain unconscious imposition in the home about certain values, morals and certain religious dimensions of which he has no understanding. He does not see any value to those things. He neither understands it nor does it make sense to him, but he is made to do those things. Though it could ruin his life in the long term, the simple sense of the street seems to make much more sense to him than the impositions of the home.

Home should not be a place to impose your culture, ideas and morals upon the child. It should be a supportive atmosphere where there is no imposition upon the child and his intelligence is encouraged. Whenever a child is confused or lost – which is very natural for someone who is growing up and beginning to be exposed to various aspects of life – his thinking is always influenced either by the street or counter-influenced by the home. Instead, if you allow him to use his own intelligence – I trust this intelligence – generally he will choose right. Yes, a few of them may go off, that is a reality in the world. Even if you try to influence them it will happen; if you do not, it may still happen. But the chances of it happening are so much lower if there is no imposition on the child at home.

If the child feels most comfortable at home, he will naturally try to spend more time there than outside. Right now, a street corner may feel like a more comfortable place for him than being at home because of the impositions in the home ground. If that discomfort is not there at home, he will not make the street corner his sanctuary. That does not mean he is not going to be exposed to the hard realities of the world. He will always be, and they will influence him in some way or the other. But always, the parent encouraging the child to learn to think for himself, to use his intelligence to see what is best for him, is the best insurance you have so that the child grows up well.

2

Friend or Foe?

**"A true friend is someone who has the courage
to tell you what shit you are, and still be loving
and nice to you."**

Questioner: *Sadhguru, what is the meaning of friendship?*

Sadhguru: You are always making friends among those who support your way of thinking, feeling, understanding, liking, and disliking. All you are seeking is some supporting substance for whatever nonsense you have made out of yourself.

It happened last winter that a tiny little bird enjoyed
the fall time a little bit too much and didn't start its

journey south early enough. It started a little late in the winter and tried to fly out, and it just froze and fell down. A cow was passing that way and it dropped a heap of dung. The dung fell right over the bird and covered it. The warmth of the dung slowly defrosted the bird and he started feeling good and started tweeting happily. A cat was going that way. It heard the tweet, looked around, and saw that the tweet was coming from inside the dung. He pushed the dung off, pulled the bird out of the dung and ate him up.

The moral of the story is, whoever heaps you up in shit need not necessarily be your enemy. Whoever pulls you out of shit need not necessarily be your friend. And above all, when you are in a heap of shit, learn to keep your mouth shut.

If you are a friend to someone, you don't have to nag them with what is wrong with them; that is not the point. But at the same time, you must have the courage to be unpopular with people. In trying to be popular with people, in trying to maintain some kind of pleasantness around you, see how much unpleasantness you have buried within you. If you bury unpleasantness, if you sow seeds of unpleasantness into the soil, you will reap fruits of unpleasantness. If you really have a friend, you must have the courage to be unpopular with him or her, and still be loving and okay with him. Right now, your friendships are always made on agreements, likes and dislikes. But even if you are apples and oranges, you can still be good friends. A true friend is someone who has the courage to tell you what shit you are, and still be loving and nice to you – that is friendship.

On a certain day, three generals from the US Army met. They were on a tour of the Grand Canyon, along with their troops. The first general wanted to brag about the courage and the spirit of obedience in his battalion, so he said, "There is no other battalion like mine. The level of courage and obedience is so high. Real courage! Let me show you an example." He boomed "Private Peter!"

Private Peter came running, "Yes, Sir!"

"You see this," the general pointed at the Grand Canyon. "I want you to just take a leap across the canyon, now!"

The man just ran, full speed and took off. Obviously, you know where he landed.

Then the second general laughed and said, "That is nothing. Look at this." He said "Trooper Higgens!"

"Yes, Sir!" Trooper Higgens arrived.

"It's an emergency! I want you to fly and go across the canyon and inform my officer there about this."

The man flapped his hands, and you know what happened.

The third general just kept quiet. The others nudged him and said, "What about yours?" And they laughed, "No courage."

Some of the general's men were loitering around, so he said, "Hey you." One of them came. The general said, "Now, look at that down below," and pointed to a swirling quick moving stream, which was just two hundred meters from a steep waterfall. He said, "I want you take this little canoe, and cross the river."

The guy looked down and said, "General, it looks like you have been on your whiskey once again. I'm not going to do such a damn stupid thing!"

The general turned to the others and said, "See, this is real courage."

Be a little more courageous in your friendships. Be ready to lose them, it is okay. At least if you care, you must do what is good for the other, not for yourself.

There was doctor I knew who was a beer drinker. When I met him he was almost seventy years of age – a big man with a big gut. Sometime ago, he used to steadily visit a friend of his. Whenever he went, the friend would serve him beer and both of them would have a drink. Whenever they had time, either his friend came over here or he went over there, whichever way. Suddenly one day, the friend met some Guru and started doing spiritual practices and gave up his beer. So the doctor went about telling me this whole story very elaborately, and said that was the end of a great friendship. Never again did he want to go to his friend's house because the man had stopped serving beer.

Lots of friendships last like this. As long as something is flowing, it is there. The moment it is gone, everything is gone.

After all, what is a friend? A friend is another confused human being like you. A friend does not mean he is a perfect human being. It is just that when two people are relaxed enough to at least approach each other sincerely, then they become friends. Your friend is as much of a mess as you are, but if two people can be in an atmosphere sincerely with each other, he becomes your friend.

∼☙∽

"Whatever you do should touch people's lives; that is all that really matters."

Questioner: *At work, whatever your role and your salary is, you are trading your time there for money. How does an individual arrive at what is a fair value for your time and the life you are giving to this business?*

Sadhguru: How much you are worth need not be seen in terms of how much you are paid. How much you are worth should be assessed in terms of what responsibilities are given to you. The privilege is not the money that you receive; the privilege is that you have been allowed to create something. Money is a means for our survival, yes, and to that extent it is necessary. However, you must always assess yourself in terms of whatever you are being asked to do. What is the level of responsibility that is being offered to you? What is the opportunity for you to create something truly worthwhile, both for yourself and for everyone around you? Any work that you do in the world is truly worthwhile for you only if you are able to touch people's lives deeply.

For example, if you were to make a film, would you want to make a film nobody wants to watch? Or build a house nobody wants to live in? You would not want to produce something nobody wants to use. So in some way, you are longing to touch people's lives. If you closely observe your life, you will see that touching people's lives with the activity you perform is important to you.

Many people are trying to divide their life into work and family – where work is something that you do just for money and family is something you do to touch people's lives. But no matter how much money you earn, if you find your husband, wife or children are not at all touched by what you do, it would suddenly seem meaningless to have a family. Somewhere in your life, you want people to be touched by what you do. This aspect need not remain or restrict itself to family alone; it could extend itself into every area of life. Whatever you do should touch people's lives; that is all that really matters.

How deeply you touch people's lives depends on how involved you are with what you do. If you are deeply involved, the way you work will naturally be very different, and according to your capabilities, you will be paid. Sometimes you will have to bargain a little or ask for a raise – perhaps your boss has forgotten that you need one. But generally, if people realize the value of what you are to that particular business or company, they will pay accordingly.

If you grow in what you are doing, some day, when it is necessary, you could shift from one position to the next, and your money could multiply a hundred times over. For example, let us say you are heading a corporation and for whatever reason you are not paid much, but you have been given full responsibility to run the whole operation. If you are performing well and the whole world is watching, tomorrow anyone will be willing to grab you for any amount. So your value need not always be gauged in terms of money.

We have established corporations so that what we cannot do individually, we can achieve collectively. We could have all operated as individual entrepreneurs – that is how we operated historically, where everyone was a manufacturer and trader of some commodity. But we are willing to put the will of thousands of people together in one direction, because the corporation wants to achieve something big.

Your real worth is a question of where you are placed in this corporation of people looking to move in one direction, and the level of responsibility and trust that has been placed in you. How much you derive from it in terms of money is not everything. Yes, it is important, but it is not everything. You must always gauge your worth in terms of the level of responsibility people are willing to give you, and whether what you are creating is truly worthwhile for yourself and for others.

"Out of this whole mass of people, if you take any human being, that person is absolutely unique!"

Questioner: *How can we love people who irritate us?*

Sadhguru: You cannot love people who irritate you; you can only pretend to love them. Instead of pretending, just see that they irritate you and look at why they irritate you. They irritate you simply because they are not the way you expect them to be, they are not the way you want them to be.

There is no point in deceiving yourself. Just see that this irritation is happening because you have already decided what is right and what is wrong. If they behave in a different way, it will irritate you first, then you will get angry, then you will hate them. These are all natural processes. It happens simply because you expect everyone in the world to be like you. If everyone in the world was like you, could you be here? If there was one more person like you in your own home, it would not be possible for you to live in there.

It is very good that everyone in the world is the way they are. Out of this whole mass of people, if you take any human being, that person is absolutely unique! There is no other human being like him anywhere on this planet. There never was one and there never will be another such person. This is an absolutely unique human being. If you recognize that there is only one person like this, that he is such precious material, how can he irritate you? There is no other human being like them. And it is such a miracle that you know this human being who is absolutely unique. If you see this, where is the question of irritation?

Only if you are simply blind to life, you will get irritated. If you open your eyes and look at life, how can anyone irritate you? The only way you will become an outpouring of love is by seeing the uniqueness of everything in creation.

"You spend more hours in your workplace than with your family or anywhere else. When this is so, is it not important that we make this into a beautiful experience?"

Questioner: *Sadhguru, in the corporate context, how do we work together in teams that are often spread across the globe, with everybody having their own cultural and other kinds of backgrounds?*

Sadhguru: When I was at the World Economic Forum, I was in a breakfast meeting with a very select group of people, and we were talking about multi-cultural leadership in the corporate sector. Today, you may be a European company but you may have a Chinese CEO; you may be an American company but you may have an Indian CEO; you maybe an Indian company but you may have an American CEO. That is how the corporate world has shifted. Where you move is just a question of your capability, not a question of your national identity. National identities are becoming loose in the world because of technology and transparency of various things.

A hundred or two hundred years ago, there were not many nations on this planet. Only a few nations had a strong identity. The rest of the human population had ethnic and religious identities. In the last 150 years, we have strived to make national identity the biggest thing. Now, whatever your ethnicity or religion maybe, you say "I am an American," or "I am an Indian." But now, that is becoming meaningless because you cannot contain people within the borders of a nation. Because of technology, Indian boys are falling in love with Pakistani girls on the internet, though there is a Line of Control! You cannot stop people because technology has made borders very transparent. You could be fighting a war in Iraq, but you may be in close relationship with somebody in Iraq on the internet. Especially in the corporate sector, national boundaries or national identities are becoming very loose. Large corporations have people from a minimum of 30 to 40 different nationalities working in the top management.

Because of cultural and a variety of differences, the very way you eat, dress, and do things is different. To function as a team and produce results can be a challenge. This was the theme of the discussion – how do you lead a multicultural group? When all of us were from one culture, it was easier to connect. Now they are from different places and backgrounds. How do you get all of them to do what needs to be done?

I was heading one small group of people there and I asked them, "Every time I enter the United States, they make me stand in a line which says 'Resident Alien.' When I look around, nobody fits the description except me! All the others look normal. I am the only one who could fit the description. Suppose someone who looked like me applied to be the CEO of your company, would you let him? Or would you be prejudiced in some way just because of the appearance?"

The moment you see a person you build prejudice about just the way he looks, the color of his skin, his clothing, his mannerism, all these things. You do not really evaluate the person for who he is. It is so funny, in the other places it does not happen so much, but in the Washington DC airport, all the security and other staff and even the immigration people, try to talk to me in sign language! They are 100% sure that there is no English written on my face. When you are boxed like this in different ways in your mind, how can you lead? Your leadership is by accident, not by any great vision or capability. People would be more likely to create something significant without a leader at all. A stupid leader can cause so much disaster that without a leader, people may do something better though it may be a little chaotic.

Essentially, what you being a leader means is that knowingly or unknowingly, you have taken the destiny of a few people into your hands. You have taken up that responsibility. A leader need not necessarily be the leader of a nation or a large group of people. If you are running a family, you are a leader. In some way, you have taken the destiny of someone's life into your hands. Anyone who is willing to take responsibility for one more life is a leader. It is just a question of the scale. People will choose the scale of leadership according to one's capabilities, but everyone is a leader in some way. At least if you have chosen to take your destiny into your hands, you are a leader. Only if you are a hobo you are not a leader.

Let me tell you a joke.

An American tourist went on a visit to England. A local person was taking him around and he showed him a certain estate and said, "Here lives an aristocrat."

The American was confused, "What was that? An astronaut?"

"No, an aristocrat."

"What is that?" the American asked.

The Englishman was unable to believe that there could be a human being who did not know what an aristocrat was. "You don't know what an aristocrat is? An aristocrat means he doesn't have to do any work. Everything comes to him one way or the other. He always has a good place somewhere. Wherever he goes, he has a ringside seat and he does nothing; he lives off other people."

"Oh, that! In America we call them hobos!"

So that's a hobo. Unless you are a hobo, in some capacity, you are a leader. Once you understand you are a leader, that means either you have taken your own destiny into your hands or maybe you have taken the destiny of a few more lives into your hands; it is a certain responsibility. If you want to lead any group of people, the first thing you must understand is they are the privileged people, not you. They have their choices, but you have no choice. Once you take up a certain responsibility, there are no choices; the choice is already made. You can't keep shifting and hopping every day. Whatever you have chosen, you have to stick to it. Hobos can skip and change every day, but once you have become a leader, either to your own life or a few more lives, then there is no shifting every day. It is very beautiful. It is a good fixer for you. Your profession is a limited space and your commitment to them is not for life, but for that limited time when you are working together, you see it through.

A major part of your life, in terms of hours per day, is probably spent in the workplace. You spend more hours in your workplace than with your family or anywhere else. When this is so, is it not important that we make this into a beautiful experience? If you see them as your own, then leading people will not be a problem. Leading a chick is not a problem for a hen. Wherever it goes, the chicks will come behind her because there is a certain assurance that she cares and loves them. If that assurance is not there, do you think those chicks would follow? You just have to do that.

"If upliftment has to happen, we need a powerful, nonsectarian spiritual process to liberate people like that, so that every human being can blossom in his own way."

Questioner: *There is a lot of violence going on in the world now and even my daughter was doing a paper on bullying in school. I find myself unable to explain to her what the source of violence is. Can you speak about this and also about what someone like myself could do to assist in solving school bullying?*

Sadhguru: The world is full of bullying. The more powerful are always bullying the less powerful. Whether it is in the form of nations, communities or individual human beings, bullying is happening everywhere, all the time. We have structured the world in such a way that if you don't learn to bully enough, at least in the society's eyes, you don't get anywhere. Either you bully on the strength of your muscle or do it in subtle ways, but bullying is happening all over the place.

The international situation is not any different from the street corner. The strong lean on the weak in so many ways. It is still a caveman's world of "survival of the fittest," but conducted in a more cunning manner.

I was visiting a certain country a few years ago and was invited to speak at the house of a well-known family there.

There was a very interesting guy there, who does nothing. He is just aristocratic – a hobo! He asked me, "How much do they pay you for visiting this country? You are here for eight days. How much do you get?"

I replied, "Nobody pays me anything nor do I earn anything. I just come because people invite me."

This person replied, "That's very suspicious! If you had asked for money, that would be straightforward. But you don't want money. People here will be very suspicious of that. If you say 'I want money,' we will deal with you. If you say 'I don't want money,' we will become very suspicious."

The way the world runs right now is by bullying. We are producing "leaders" in the school. Those who bully well could become leaders tomorrow! We have not produced the right kind of leaders – bullies are considered leaders. Compassionate human beings with a larger vision for humanity are not considered leaders; they are considered philosophers in this world. They are dismissed off as visionaries.

The leaders are always bullies who know how to elbow their way through everything and then fist you down in some way. We have set up a system like that in the world, everywhere. This has to change, but it won't happen overnight. It needs lots of work on individual human beings. General statements and slogans on the street will not help. It needs pointed work on individual human beings. There has not been enough infrastructure to do that kind of work.

As a part of this, Isha is in the process of starting a leadership academy. The vision for this is to develop leaders on all levels. A weekend "Management and Leadership Course" for housewives, and a week-long management course for local entrepreneurs, whether a vegetable vendor or shop owner.

Another thing we are doing is building infrastructure for an inclusive consciousness. In India, such infrastructure was there in plenty in the past, but nothing has been done in the last few hundred years. This infrastructure is completely missing in most parts of the world. Everything is oriented towards survival, but there is nothing for a human being to become a full-fledged human being who has blossomed.

Children bully because they perceive that the world works this way. Everybody is using whatever power they have to beat someone else down. People are not using the power they have to uplift someone. Even if they uplift someone, there is a string attached that they can pull you down any time they want.

Nobody wants you to be a hydrogen balloon, let you loose and say "rise." They have a string attached to it.

If upliftment has to happen, we need a powerful, nonsectarian spiritual process to liberate people like that, so that every human being can blossom in his own way. He need not be my way or your way. He can blossom in his own way as long as he is inclusive as life is. Inclusiveness is not an ideology, or some kind of a philosophy. Inclusiveness is a way of life. Life is inclusive. The existence is happening out of its inclusiveness, not out of exclusiveness. Not a single atom can exist here exclusively.

If you go up into high altitudes, your body starts losing its integrity, in the sense, for your body to retain its shape and form, you need a certain amount of pressure supporting you. I am talking in the most basic terms – if you keep rising and the pressure decreases, at a certain point your body will disintegrate. Right now, you are constantly being supported by everything to retain your form. So, you being exclusive is ridiculous. Bullying is not because someone is evil. Once we breed exclusiveness, bullying is natural. Inclusiveness is the only answer. Inclusiveness is not in terms of, "I love you, you love me." It is about experientially seeing that life is an inclusive process. There is no other way to be.

If at least ten percent of humanity strives hard, we could create a *strong* sense of inclusiveness on the planet in their lifetime – not absolute, but a strong sense. Right now, not even a fraction of one percent is striving for it, so it seems like a very remote possibility, but that could change.

3

Cosmic Connect

∽◐↝

"The very nature of how this biological body gets created is very directly connected to the nature of the earth, the sun, and the moon."

Today, modern science is realizing that there is nothing in the existence which can be separated from something else. Everything is in connection with everything else. The whole cosmos is a composite happening; it is not an exclusive happening. You are not an exclusive life, the planet is not an exclusive planet, and the solar system is not an exclusive system. We may not be able to figure out where this existence begins or where it ends, but today, we know that everything that can be is in some way connected; it is not happening in exclusivity. The word "yoga" means "union" – it is all in one happening. It is just for you to realize that it is so.

What we refer to as "mysticism" is essentially a way to know your own nature, and know the relationship between yourself and the cosmos, to know and to realize there is no such thing as "me and the cosmos" – there is just me, there is just cosmic reverberation. To know this, not as knowledge, deduction, philosophy or ideology, but as a living reality, is mysticism.

It is very important to realize that you have a deep relationship with anything that reverberates in this existence. Particularly, the nature of life on this planet is very strongly imprinted with the qualities of the solar *mandala* or the solar system. There are six minor influences, but three – the earth, the sun, and the moon – are very prominent; they almost cover everything. Our birth and our lives here are very deeply connected with these three. The very nature of how this biological body gets created is very directly connected to the nature of the earth, the sun, and the moon.

Even very remote societies which did not see too much civilization or culture evolving out of them – societies where no great amount of spiritual process happened – even they could not miss the connection and the influence of the earth, the moon and the sun upon the human system. Of course, at least nobody could miss how the cycles of the moon and the feminine body are connected, which is very directly connected to the making of this physical body.

Yoga revolves around these three dimensions – about mastering the energy of the sun, the moon, and being in tune with the earth – because fundamentally, your life is empowered by these three forces. All life upon this planet is solar powered, we are here now only because our mothers' bodies were in-sync with the lunar cycles, and there is a very direct connection between the way the planet spins and what happens in the human system on many different levels.

The human body, human energies, human possibilities, and human destiny are so deeply entwined with the spin of the planet. If one does not understand and is not in tune with the law that governs this, they will be spinning eternally. You know, if you spin around for sometime, then you don't know where you are going! This is the state of most human beings, because they are unknowingly spinning with the planet and they don't know where they are going.

For example, the earth's equator is divided into 360 degrees, and each degree is further divided into what are referred to as minutes. There are sixty minutes in every degree. One minute accounts for one nautical mile, so the circumference of the earth at the equator is 21,600 nautical miles. If you look at how many breaths you take per day, if you are not in a state of heavy excitement, you will be taking fifteen breaths per minute. If you have done lots of *sadhana*,[2] then you could be taking twelve breaths per minute, otherwise, if you are healthy and well,

---

[2] Spiritual practices which are used as a means to realization.

you will be taking fifteen. Fifteen breaths per minute means 900 breaths an hour, or 21,600 breaths a day, and that's the circumference of the earth in nautical miles! So if the planet is not spinning on time, it is not good at all for us. And if you are not in tune with it, it is still no good for you.

Similarly, there are 114 major *chakras*[3] in the system. Out of these, two are outside the physical body. Of the remaining 112, only 108 can actually be worked upon; the remaining four just flower as a consequence. The number 108 has manifested in the human system because it is a significant number in the making of the solar system. The ratio of the diameter of the sun and the distance between the earth and the sun is 108 times. The ratio of the diameter of the moon and the distance between the earth and the moon is 108 times. The ratio of the diameter of the earth and the diameter of the sun is 108 times. And hence, 108 is significant in various spiritual practices. This is why if you wear a *rudraksh*,[4] it has 108 beads, people chant 108 mantras, and so many other things because the human system is built like this in alignment with the cosmic system.

If you look at the orbit of the earth as it goes around the sun, in yogic astrology, we divide this into twenty-seven segments. These twenty-seven segments are known as *nakshatras*. Each of these nakshatras is divided in four parts, totally representing

---

[3]   Lit.wheel. Also refers to the junctions of nadis in the pranic body.

[4]   Sacred beads. Seeds of a tree (*Elaeocarpus ganitrus*) found mostly in the Himalayan region.

108 units. These twenty-seven play a significant role upon the planet. They represent the phases of the moon. As the planet travels from one nakshatra to the next, the moon completes half a circle. As the earth goes to the next nakshatra, the moon completes the circle. So, each segment represents the transition from a *Purnima* (full moon) to an *Amavasya* (new moon), and from an Amavasya to a Purnima. As this is happening, the human cycles within the human body respond and correspond to it.

This is very obvious in a woman's system. About every twenty-seven days, a cycle should happen in a woman's body, if she has to be perfectly healthy. In the male body, it is not so obvious and manifest, but it is happening in a different way, and the cycle is of a larger span. Because it is of a larger span and men don't have much arithmetic capabilities, they don't count when their last cycle was! This is mainly because of arithmetic problems, but otherwise this is happening.

Your body has to be in-sync with the solar system to function at its optimum. Every practice that is taught in yoga always takes into consideration the cycles of the sun, the moon and variations that occur, because it is in collaboration with all three that this body is created. There is a certain synchronicity and alignment between the human system and the universal movement. Yoga means to get your system aligned, so that a different dimension of life becomes possible for you. If you just learn to hold your body right, everything that is worth knowing is right here. You can download the cosmos into you. The human system is a very complex system. There is no machine comparable to this, and no technology beyond this. This is the highest level of technology, but you are handling it like a blacksmith's anvil.

If you are a blacksmith and we gave you a fine computer, what would you do? You would start hammering at it. That is not the way to operate a computer. This body is, physically, the highest level of technology you can create in this universe, but you are trying to handle it in a crude manner. That's all the problem is. You have to pay enormous attention to this. Only then it will yield. You need to understand this: nothing in this existence will yield to you if you do not pay attention to it. And there is nothing in this existence, which will not yield to you, if you are willing to pay attention to it. If you pay the right kind of attention, everything has to yield.

"Are you looking for wellbeing, or are you looking for liberation; that is the question. Accordingly, you must live."

Questioner: *Sadhguru, in our life, the same pattern of things keeps happening over a period of time. The same kind of emotion, the same kind of situation, how do we come out of that pattern?*

Sadhguru: It's good that you noticed that the same patterns are happening and repeating themselves. Most people do not even see that. They keep repeating the same cycles in different scenery and they think they are okay. Life's scenery will anyway change. The last time some rubbish happened to you, you were in school. The next time it happened to you, you were in college, so the scenery was different. The next time it happened to you, you were in a job. The next time, you were married. But if you closely observe your life, you will see that the same things are happening.

Suppose you are going to Coimbatore from the Isha Yoga Center and you pass Iruttupallam.[5] You look around and move on. As you are driving happily, Iruttupallam came again. "Oh, Iruttupallam again? Okay, bad luck." You keep driving and after some time, Iruttupallam came again – must be coincidence. If Iruttupallam comes another time, you must know that you are not going anywhere – you are going in circles.

If you are looking at human life as just the body, then yes, the body is getting somewhere. Where is your body going? To the grave. Every moment, the body is getting closer to the grave. If you exist here as a physical entity, that is all that is happening. You will see, life will be a play, then it becomes pleasure, then it becomes so many things, then every joint hurts, and then it gets terrified because it is coming to an end. This is the progression of physical life. You do not have to go through it to

---

5   A small town near the Isha Yoga Center.

know it. You have enough intelligence to sit here and see it. Our fortune is that we are not limited to the physical; we have other dimensions to us. In terms of your mental status and emotional status, either they can continue to grow or they can go in circles. You may not be aware yet of other dimensions, but even there you can either go in cycles or you can go somewhere.

When you say, "I notice that my life is going in cycles," you are essentially talking about the situations around you. More than that, you are talking about your own mental and emotional states going through the same cycles. Women cannot miss these cycles; they can notice that this is happening to them. Unfortunately, men do not have menstrual cycles. I am saying unfortunately because if there was such a strong reminder, you would not miss it. Men have to be much more aware; they need to do much more work because otherwise, you will think you are going somewhere, but you are only going to Iruttupallam. Physiologically there is a strong reminder in the female body. This strong reminder is not a curse. It is a blessing if you know how to use it, because any volatile, destabilized situation is a possibility for change. When there is a set process, you cannot change things so easily. When there is a periodic destabilization of the system, there is a great possibility for change.

If you are going through cycles, if you are a very balanced man, your cycles will happen once in twelve or twelve-and-a-quarter years. If you are not so balanced, it will happen in a quarter of that time – you will face this every three years or a little over three years. If you are not even that balanced, it may happen much more often – every sixteen to eighteen months. If your cycles come below three months, you shouldn't be here – you should be in a mental asylum. For sure, you are dangerous for yourself and everyone around you. You should be either dulled by medicine, or chained to a bed because your cycles are so short, you will become dangerously volatile.

If you do not stand up with a certain level of awareness and determination, and a sense of going somewhere, you will naturally become part of the cycles because everything in this solar system is definitely cyclical – there are various kinds of cycles happening. You could become a part of the longest cycle that is happening here that is relevant to human life, which is one hundred and forty-four years. Once in one hundred and forty-four years, certain things happen in the solar system. This is why we have a *Maha Kumbha Mela* once every one hundred and forty-four years. The next cycle is twelve-and-a-quarter years. The others are much shorter. These cycles can mean bondage or they can also mean transcendence. You can transcend from one cycle of life to another, or you can repeat the same cycle. That depends on who *you* are.

The difference between astrology and spirituality is this: astrology is trying to tell you how these cycles bind you and that this is the only way to live, while a spiritual process is telling you how you can get away from these cycles. We are not denying the cycles. That would be stupid. The cycles are definitely there, but we are looking at the possibilities of how you can slip away from these cycles. That is the difference. If you live here conscious of the cycles, your life will have a certain equanimity, and a certain level of success, prosperity and wellbeing. If you are constantly looking at how to become free from the cycle, you are looking for your liberation. Are you looking for just wellbeing or are you looking for liberation? That is the question. Accordingly, you must live.

If your life is going in cycles and you are repeatedly coming to Iruttupallam, and if you understand that you are not going to reach anywhere like this, it is time to change the pattern. I want you to observe, is it happening once in three months, once in nine months, once in sixteen to eighteen months, once in three to three-and-a-quarter years, or is it happening once in twelve years? Do not start imagining all kinds of things, but it is happening. Whether you are able to notice it or not, it is happening. It is not happening only with your mental and emotional situations. If you are conscious, even physical situations around you will repeat themselves. It is so uncanny that even physical situations happen exactly the same way.

Have you heard people say, "A snake's memory is for twelve years"? It is very common among Kannada and Telugu people. They say "A snake's vengeance is for twelve years. If you hurt it, it will remember for twelve years and come and bite you." It is not that the cobra remembers for twelve years. The cobra goes through certain cycles and it is connected with the serpent within us. I am saying the serpent within us because the core part of your brain is a reptilian brain. Now you know why you are so venomous! This reptilian brain naturally makes you available to this twelve-and-a-quarter-year cycle of the sun because all reptiles are very strongly associated with that cycle. Because a snake is strongly associated with that cycle and there is a twelve-year cycle in your own brain, the snake reminds you.

What can you do about your cycles? They need not manifest with such regularity. If it is manifesting every three months, we can push it to nine months. If it is manifesting every nine months, we can push it to eighteen months. If it is eighteen months, we can push it to three years. Or we can push it to twelve years, or we can push it to one hundred and forty-four years. Or above all, instead of trying to dodge these cycles, we can ride these cycles.

"You must sincerely look at yourself – don't worry about the social impact, you don't have to admit it to anybody – within yourself, aren't you quite insane?"

Questioner: *Namaskaram. What does the path of brahmacharya[6] involve? And how can one know if he is capable of that?*

---

[6] The path of the divine. A life of celibacy and studentship on the path of spirituality.

Sadhguru: Brahmacharya means to be like the breeze – that is, you don't stick to anything. The breeze is going everywhere, but we don't know where it is coming from right now. It just crossed the oceans and came, here it is, and it keeps going. Brahmacharya means simply being life; to live the way you were born – alone. Even if your mother happened to bear twins, you were still born alone. So brahmacharya means to be in a very close association with the Divine – to live like that.

Brahmacharya is not a great step; it is just to exist as life is. Marriage is a great step – you are trying to do something, very big! At least, people believe so. Brahmacharya means you did nothing, you allowed your life to happen. Just the Creator made you, you don't make anything out of it.

So there is no step. If you don't do anything, you are a brahmachari. But there is sadhana, there are other disciplines, what is that about? That is only to help you stay like that because once you picked up material from this planet, the qualities of this planet will enter you and try to rule you. One basic quality is that once you pick up earth, there is something called inertia. Even to wake up in the morning there is inertia, isn't it? To be on the path of the Divine means not to give in to the way of the earth. One thing is inertia, another thing is the compulsive movement. If you pick up a piece of this earth, you become like the earth. It tries to take you in circles. Cyclical movement is the basis of everything that you call as physical in the universe.

If you move in a circle, however large the circle is, you always come back. Even if you are not invited! We don't know whether the world wants you or not, but you will anyway come back because you are on a circle. Those who have realized that they are not really wanted around here, those who want to be on a straight path, for them, it is the path of the Divine, not the planetary trajectory. One takes brahmacharya as a path and a discipline instead of as a natural process, so that they don't get into the cyclical motion of life. They don't want to succumb to this.

What does it involve? If you are very conscious, it involves nothing, it is very simple. You wake up every day in the morning like you were just born, you go to sleep like you would die. In between, whatever is useful to everyone you do, because you have still not reached that place where you can exist without activity – you need to do something. The idea is that the activity should be never about you, because if it is, you will pile up entanglement. So, you constantly do activity which is not about you. You do so much activity, that when you go to bed you don't have a moment – you fall like you are dead. Then you wake up before the birds and get busy. The rest will be taken care of by Grace. You need not do too much because we invest a certain amount of energy to "manufacture" a brahmachari. Actually, it shouldn't be necessary. If they simply didn't do anything, they would be there, but the ways of the earth rule from within because after all, you can't keep your body down – it has memory, it has a huge karmic pile, so it has its tendencies.

These tendencies are not natural to your being, but this vehicle – the body – tends to go like this. Suppose you are driving a car which has a small alignment problem. You have to straighten it, otherwise it will keep pulling one way. The body also has an alignment problem, and it always wants to go like this. Once it bends or turns, it is just a question of time before it completes the circle. But because it is taking a certain period of time and one's awareness is not in any great place, every time you pass the same spot it looks like a new place. If you sit somewhere in the afternoon, the whole place looks in one way. If you sit there during sunset, it looks different. If you come at midnight, it looks different. So, you think you have come to a different place every time but no, it is just a question of time, season and short memory.

A dis-aligned vehicle or a vehicle which is attuned to go in circular motion is what you have. Whether you are doing a twelve-year cycle or a three-month cycle, the difference is only a question of percentages of madness. If you are doing a three-month cycle, everyone can see that you are mad. If you are doing twelve-year cycles, people don't make out, but if you are sincere, you know you are crazy. The only thing is you can fool the world into thinking you are okay.

You must sincerely look at yourself – don't worry about the social impact, you don't have to admit it to anyone – within yourself, aren't you quite insane? I want you to sincerely look at this. If you are sincere and straight about yourself, you know you are quite *off.* If you have admitted this to yourself and want to fix it, but you have become so much of a social being that *how you are* doesn't matter, *how you look* is all that matters to you – then you can go on for many lifetimes. If how you are matters to you, if your being has become very important for you and not what someone thinks about you, if it is not another person's opinion which is crafting your life but the nature of your being, then you will naturally be on the path of the Divine. You will *want* to be there. There is no other way.

"For everything that nature and people around you are providing, shouldn't you bow down to everything in absolute gratitude?"

Questioner: *Sadhguru, today is the first day of spring, and it is celebrated as Mother's Day in Lebanon. Can you please say something about mothers?*

Sadhguru: If this is the official beginning of spring, that means it is Mother Earth's day, not your mother's day, because your mother can deliver any time. Nature, thinking that he has enough intelligence, gave this freedom to a human being that he is not seasonal. The population on the planet says that nature over-estimated human intelligence! So, if it is the beginning of spring, it is definitely Mother Earth's day, because this is the time she gets into movement; this is the time life bursts forth.

Talking about Mother Earth... in the body that you carry right now, that which came out of your mother's womb is hardly there – it is mostly gone. Today, whatever the number of kilograms you carry, it is all from Mother Earth. I am not trying to belittle the genetic or biological mother; it is just that if you are a spiritual seeker, it is extremely important you get the right perspective of everything. If you exaggerate things in your mind or with your emotion, you will point yourself in wrong directions and waste a huge amount of time and life. If you love someone, you will exaggerate, if you hate someone, you exaggerate. If you like someone, you exaggerate, if you dislike someone, you will exaggerate. Exaggeration means, either unconsciously or intentionally, you are deviating from truth. Deviating from truth means you are working against yourself. One who works against himself does not need an enemy. This is called self-help! That is the beauty of your life – you are completely self-reliant.

So, what do I have to say about mothers? We are grateful and we appreciate both – our biological mothers and Mother Earth. We are here because of this mother and that mother. Every day of your life, you should appreciate all the things and all the people who are contributing to make your life what it is today. When you wake up in the morning, the first thing is to be grateful that you are still alive because from the time you went to sleep till the time you woke up in the morning, thousands of people did not wake up on the planet. But we woke up. Isn't it great? Shouldn't there be gratitude?

"Whom should I be grateful to?" Just look at how many forces are working to keep you in place and keep you alive. The planet itself is like a pressurized compartment maintaining the perfect pressure. This isn't happening because someone is using a remote control and controlling it. Everything that is needed for your wellbeing is being taken care of by the Creator. I want you to understand you are floating in nothingness; you are not standing on solid ground as you believe. The damn solid ground is floating in nothingness and nobody knows the depth of that nothingness and still every day it spins, every day the sun comes up, every day your life goes on. Shouldn't you be grateful? Every moment, every step that you take, the planet is not giving in and breaking up. Every breath that you take, the air is not escaping from the atmosphere and denying you. You don't have to think of all these things every moment, but one must be conscious that this life is not conducted by you. You did not give birth to this; the one who gave birth, you call her the "mother," the one who caused it, you call him the "father," but all these millions of motherly or fatherly forces are working every moment of your life. You did not ask and you are not paying a bill for all these. Simply, everything is provided. So, for everything that nature and people around you are providing, shouldn't you bow down to everything in absolute gratitude? Because you are incapable of conducting your life without all these forces cooperating with you, without even being asked.

If you don't appreciate this, if you have lost your consciousness completely, it is because you are too busy with some rubbish that is happening in your head. That is the only reason anybody can miss all this. Something that is happening in your head is important because you think too much of yourself.

So let's make every day Mother's Day, what is the problem? If you look at it closely enough, there isn't one thing in creation without which you can exist. Look upon everything as a mother. Today is the tree-mother's day, tomorrow is the mountain-mother's day, the next day is your biological mother's day.

The reason why these days have been fixed is because otherwise people will never think of their mother. Cultures have become like this. But if you are a little more conscious, if you remind yourself and look, "The tree is giving me oxygen. They are supporting me every moment." If you recognize this with everything, everywhere that you walk, you will become conscious. If you are so unconscious that you have no thought for what nourishes you and what will ultimately deliver you, it is better you live as per these days – at least you know you are just a pig. I am not using the word "pig" in any derogatory way. A pig has a great appetite, he can eat well and grunt – it is a quality by itself. A pig celebrates Mother's Day and believes that it is conscious because once a year it is marked, "Today is Mother's Day, let us be grateful to the mothers, let's write a card to the mother." I would say it is better to forget about your mother and one day suddenly when life knocks on your head you will anyway remember – that may be more useful than fixing a day to remember your mother – rather than give you a false sense of awareness and gratitude.

On one of these Mother's Days, it happened in the United States with a certain old lady who was a grandmother. All the children and grandchildren are supposed to come and visit the grandparents, but as the grandchildren grow up, they become teenagers and don't want to come. But the grandmother always sends a gift to them. They are happy because anyway the gift is coming. They don't want to go and see her; the old woman, who wants to go and see her? For two or three years none of the grandchildren turned up. So the next year when Mother's Day came, the daughter went to visit the old lady, but the grandchildren didn't turn up. The daughter apologized, "None of my children are willing to come and even see you once a year. I am sorry."

But the old lady was in a very chirpy mood and said, "Don't worry, this year all of them will come."

The daughter asked, "How are you so sure?"

The old lady said "Instead of sending them gifts, I sent them gift cheques this time."

"So? Why will they come?"

The old lady replied, "I didn't sign them."

4

Beyond Life and Death

∽◈∽

"Relationships are an opportunity to achieve some kind of union which will pave the way for a greater possibility."

There is a dimension of relationship which is not of the body or physicality, which is not of companionship or emotional proximity, but simply of basic life energy. If your sense of body, mind and emotions recede to a very minor aspect, you are generally a large sphere of energy. Then you could fit perfectly well and for good. When I say for good, it could be taken beyond life and death. It is in this context that the traditions always held the relationship between a Guru and a *shishya*, or disciple as of the highest order. Not because they love each other more than you loved your child or your husband, but because these three aspects – body, mind and emotion – which are essentially individualistic, have been kept aside. Now it fits. If a relationship is formed on the level of your energy, it does not matter which part of the world you are in, I can still have you shaking, I can still have a certain intimacy which is not possible even if you live with someone for fifty years.

Even on the level of your energy, if you look at it on the surface, each individual energy has its own flavor and they can never match. But the fundamental aspect of the energy is same. If you are capable of penetrating that individual flavor and touching another dimension which is universal in nature, it is in instant rapport. It does not need any conversation or any kind of transaction. It is just a union.

Relationships are not about compatibility, companionship or about extracting happiness from each other. Relationships are an opportunity to achieve some kind of union which will pave the way for a greater possibility. If that does not happen, a relationship is more of an encumbrance and hurdle than anything else because when you hold relationships, you become even more exclusive.

The only way you can become free is to become inclusive. People always understand freedom as, "I will do what I want to do. I will be where I want to be." People understand freedom as exclusiveness. If you become exclusive, you will become a bondage by yourself. Your very existence will become bondage.

The more exclusive you make yourself in your thought and emotion, the more excluded from the life process you become.

The only way you can know freedom is by inclusion. The fundamental dimension is inclusion; inclusion not in terms of "I love you, you love me." That may be needed on the surface to make you willing, but love is a solvent, not a solution. It dissolves the rough edges in you and brings you a little closer to people so that there is a possibility. But it is not the real thing.

When you hold a relationship with someone, the closer it is, the more excluded from the rest of the world you become, because now you have a party to your exclusiveness. You have formed a small clique where you do not have to look out at all. Especially if it is going well, then you become completely excluded from the rest. It is not going to take a human being to a better place. It can only take him to a more entangled situation in life.

If you do not consciously evolve your ability to form relationships with everything around you on that dimension where there is a natural union, you will never know the joy of being in this world. You will only know the fear and anxiety of being in this world. If you know this union with everything around you, just to be in this world can be an absolutely, incredibly ecstatic process. If you can just look at the mountain and burst into tears, if you can look at an insect, and not feel love but just feel it as a part of yourself, if you understand the intensity of life that is happening, that intensity is an explosion which will not allow you to be exclusive; it will naturally make you all inclusive.

"If you become an empty page and remain one, you can project life upon it."

Every creature here, however small or big, is continually in a relationship with the rest of creation and also with the source of creation. If there already is an inevitable relationship, what is there to do? Just change the quality of the relationship. You can sit here cursing this planet or you can sit here blessing this planet because it is giving you a piece of place to sit down upon. It is a big difference in the way you hold the relationship.

It is about changing the relationship. If the relationship is only on a physical level, you will know certain things. If it is mental, you will know other things. If it is emotional, you will know different kinds of things. But you will still not know what it is. Do you see, from the moment of your birth till now, many things about your body have changed and are continuing to change? Similarly, many things about your mind and emotion are changing and continuing to change. Even if you have "frozen" it, still it is changing.

In a way, the whole spiritual process is about changing your relationship with the existence from being just one of body, mind and emotion, to a subtler dimension of existence. All knowing comes just from this.

It is like this:

A scoundrel is knowledgeable
A fool will know
But a sage is an empty page

Because a sage is an empty page, just about anything can be grasped. If you already wrote something else upon it, it would be confusion.

All the big, elaborate and confusing talk about karma that is going on just means that you are not an empty page. Too much is written already so whatever else is written is going to be lost. It does not matter what is written on a page which is already full of stuff; whatever you write and however valuable what you write is, it is going to be missed. That is why in this country, people look at you and say, "Karma."

All the spiritual sadhana is not to become knowledgeable, but to become an empty page so that anything can be projected. If you become an empty page and remain one, you can project life upon it. If you have been to the local theater, any number of movies have been played upon that screen, but it does not distort anything because light is a subtle thing. If they had used a crayon or a paint brush, those screens would have been discarded a long time ago.

So it is about moving your relationship with the existence from that which is physical, mental, and emotional – which will leave marks and never allow you to have an empty page – into an etheric state, where your relationship is far deeper and much more profound, but subtle in such a way that you can play any kind of cinema on it. The moment it is off, it is off – not a trace left. If the previous movie left even a little bit of trace upon the screen, the next movie would be a disaster. That is all that is happening right now. The previous movies have left impressions.

Are you ready for a joke?

Shankaran Pillai went to the United States. He was sightseeing in Washington D.C. Particularly when you go on tour and when you go sightseeing, for many couples, that is when big arguments happen because the wife wants to express all the suppressed aspirations at that time. She wants to do this, she wants to see that, she wants to eat this, she wants to go here. Suddenly the husband is having problems with this new woman. This couple was walking on two sides of the street. As usual some long-haired people were protesting against the war in Iraq. Always there is some war and so, "Make love, not war"

boards are everywhere in the city. Shankaran Pillai
went and looked at it. He said, "Get married, you'll
have both."

You just have to change your relationship with the existence
and with the Creator. How? You need to understand, this is not
a relationship of choice. Whichever way, you *have* to hold a
relationship, you cannot help it. Can you sit here not connected
with any aspect of creation or Creator? You may be unaware of
it, but there is no way – unless you transcend everything that
is physical absolutely. Otherwise, whichever way you sit, stand,
or sleep, you are holding a relationship. You don't have to try to
hold a relationship. So fifty percent of the problem is solved. The
other half is very simple – you do not make too much of yourself.

I am not offering a teaching; I am only giving a method. Do
you know the distinction between the two? A teaching can be
analyzed and understood. A method has to simply be used. It
cannot be analyzed or understood. This is just a method. It does
not take much effort. You need to constantly see how small a
creature you are in this existence.

Look at the mountain and see how small you are, look at the
sky and see how small you are. Look at the distance into the
sky and see how poor your vision is. Like this, put yourself into
the right place. I am not saying depreciate yourself, I am saying
be realistic as to who the hell you are in this Creation. You do

not have to appreciate or depreciate, you do not have to lie to yourself. Simply see what is your place in the existence and constantly keep reminding yourself, "This is all I am, a speck of nothing in nothing." Who the hell you are, what you think of yourself, your greatness – these do not mean anything. Even if you disappear tomorrow morning, the whole world will be fine. This is so for you, this is so for me, this is so for everyone. The more people do not understand this, the more idiotic their lives will be. The more they come to terms with it, the more intelligently they will live.

Intelligence is not about being intellectual. There are intellectual people and there are intelligent people. Intellectuals are knowledgeable. Intelligence is not about being knowledgeable. I know too much nonsense has been fed into you, especially if you come from Western societies. They told you, "God is love." You don't know for sure, isn't it? If life is buggering you, then you will think, "God is torture." If life is going well, you think, "God is love." You do not know whether he is love or compassion or all the other nonsense that people talk about him. But if you look at every atom, every cell, every leaf, every tree, every creature, at just about everything in this creation, one thing is manifest – that he is super-intelligent. His love is not manifest. Your neighbors could be loving, but you do not want to acknowledge them, so you say God is love. You do not know about the Creator's love affair, but you cannot miss his intelligence. Wherever you see, the Creator's intelligence is manifest. With all these brains of ours, after so many millions of years of evolution, we cannot even put one atom together.

Intelligence is one single quality which is manifest in every possible way. And if you look at this intelligence, one of the foremost qualities of this intelligence is, it is a non-discriminatory intelligence. Discrimination comes to you because of intellect. Intelligence is non-discriminatory. If you just get this one thing going within you that you are non-discriminatory, it does not matter whether someone is big or small – you look at them the same way. Someone is a man, someone is a woman – you look at them the same way. Someone is God and someone is demon – you look at them the same way. A mountain and a molehill, you look the same way.

If you constantly practice this, that you see everything as the same thing, that is devotion – you bow down to whatever you see. To God also you do the same thing, to someone else also you do the same thing. You see a cow, you see a tree, you do the same thing – because devotion is a non-discriminatory intelligence. If you become a discriminatory intelligence, then you are moving further away from that which is the Creator and becoming one little fragment of creation; you become a speck of creation – a speck which is bloated within itself, thinking it is too big. You are really nothing and you are not worth anything. In this cosmos, if the whole planet disappears tomorrow it means nothing. It is that insignificant.

If you become a non-discriminatory intelligence, you are getting closer to the Creator act – to that which is the source of creation. There are five layers of the body – physical body, mental body, energy body, etheric body, and the bliss body. Getting closer to that which is the source of creation means, you are moving from physical to mental, mental to energy, energy to etheric, and then, to that which is the source of creation. When you come to the etheric space, your ability to know and perceive is greatly enhanced because you are no longer limited by the physical manifestations. What you call as "time and space" is essentially a physical manifestation. If there was no physicality, space and time would not mean anything. Only because there is physicality, there is something called as the beginning and the ending. Because there is a beginning and ending, there are measurements of time in between. If there was no physical existence, there would be no such thing as big and small. If there is no such thing as big and small, there would be no such thing as space.

These two realities of time and space are what humanity is right now experiencing as life and death. Only because there is time, there is life and there is death. Only because there is space, there is something called as you and me, this and that. Changing the relationship means, everything is just *this and this*.

∽ೖೕ∾

"If you are not attached to your body, you are not attached to any-body."

Questioner: *Can I attain mukti or liberation while remaining in a marital relationship? Because people get very attached to one another in a marriage.*

Sadhguru: In any relationship, there is attachment. Most people know relationships only as attachments. This attachment is not with the other person. Your attachment to your husband or your wife is not a big thing; you are attached because you have no other way. If you had some other way, the attachment would drop. Don't think that giving up your husband or your wife is a very great thing. If the person whom you are attached to suddenly becomes distasteful, your attachment would evaporate. If you don't like that person due to some act they do or something they say, your attachment disappears.

This must be clearly understood. The attachment is not with somebody; the attachment is with *your* body. Because you are deeply attached to *this* body, you get attached to somebody. You don't have to work on your attachments with people around you; you really need to work with your attachment to your own body. As you release yourself from this, you are free from everything.

The sense of body is so big in the human mind. The purpose of a spiritual process is to transcend that because that is the greatest trap. Your identification with the body is the basis of your entanglement with every other body. If you are not entangled with this body, you are not entangled with anybody. In sex-based relationships, where this body is involved between two people, the attachment always deepens. On the spiritual path, people are talking about brahmacharya or not getting into these kinds of relationships, not because they are against relationships and the biology of life, but only because such a relationship deepens the attachment.

What kind of relationships you hold and what you are doing in your life is in one sense irrelevant. But in another sense of creating the necessary supports, it is relevant. Whether we want to create a supportive situation for ourselves or not could vary from person to person. Some people need this kind of relationship to ground them a little bit. Otherwise they would be too disturbed to seek anything in their life. If you are capable of flying, it is beautiful. But when you are not capable of flying and if you are not grounded, you will be lost. It is a kind of grounding – it holds you down. If you look at it, in one way it is a reverse process, but right now it could be useful to you depending upon what stage of life you are in.

I want you to look at it straight – why are you seeking a certain relationship? Don't give it all kinds of meanings which do not exist. You are seeking it because by yourself, you are lost – you need support psychologically and emotionally. You are seeking it because that is the only way you know how to handle your fears and struggles within yourself. These kinds of relationships only create more struggle and conflict externally. But because you don't know how to handle your interiority, you are using the external to handle your interior. That will only be a stop-gap arrangement. It will never work forever for anyone – it cannot.

These relationships have got nothing to do with your spiritual process. Spirituality is something that you do within yourself. How you want to manage your outside is left to you, but as the internal changes, the internal also will naturally show in the exterior. But if you want to manage a certain level of exteriority and want to keep something going, it is up to you what you do with your outside.

"If a relationship transcends the physical limitations, there is a possibility of this relationship extending beyond lifetimes or across lifetimes."

Questioner: *You said some relationships can be taken beyond life and death. Can a relationship between the master and disciple in a previous birth be carried for lifetimes?*

Sadhguru: Yes. Definitely. Generally this is the only

relationship which can be carried for lifetimes. The work continues. Husbands and wives, lovers, coming together again for lifetimes because their love was so strong, is rare. Generally it is the master-disciple relationship which gets carried for lifetimes. All the other relationships come together for convenience. Once it is over, it just breaks apart.

The possibility of a relationship extending beyond lifetimes or across lifetimes comes only if the relationship transcends the physical limitations. When I say "physical," I am referring to the mental and emotional structures also as physical. Generally it is only the guru-disciple relationship which extends this way, though there could be a few examples of other relationships going beyond the physical limitations. This is because the guru-disciple relationship is for *always*. Even if the disciple has no idea of the guru's being, the guru's business is only with the disciple's being. This relationship is always energy-based. It is not emotion-based, mind-based, or body-based.

An energy-based relationship does not even realize whether the bodies have changed or if it is the same body. It just continues till the energy reaches dissolution. There is no rebirth for the energy; it is only the body which is reborn. The energy just continues as one flow and accordingly carries the relationship also as such. So, definitely this is one relationship which is carried on.

∾ର๛

"A Guru is not someone who holds a torch and shows something to you. He is the torch. He burns."

Questioner: *So if someone had a Guru in a previous lifetime and now they are sitting here with you, then what happened to their Guru?*

Sadhguru: If someone had a Guru in their past life, and they are sitting here now, then obviously it has not worked. If they had a Guru, they would not be here today. Maybe those people went to many places, and heard discourses and scholarly expositions, but they have not had a Guru. If they had a Guru and they are here, they are my people; otherwise they cannot be here.

You need to understand what you are talking about. A Guru is not someone who shows you something. The difference between a teacher or a scholar and a Guru is, a teacher or a scholar is someone who holds a torch to something and shows it to you. Because of them you might have seen something. A Guru is not someone who holds a torch and shows something to you. He *is* the torch. He burns. Either you burn with him or you do not. If you did not burn with him, that means you never had a Guru. Maybe you just went around. There are ticks in the forest; they have even gotten into me, but I am not their Guru. My blood flows through their veins, but I am not their Guru. Do you understand?

The question of someone having a Guru and now being here – there is no such drama. A Guru means it is curtains, end of drama. If you want drama you should not go to a Guru. When you want to close the drama that is when you go to the Guru. He is not a pointer, he is the point. It is very different. None of the people here had a Guru, that is why they are here. Or if they had, it was me. That is why they are here, not otherwise.

Questioner: *So if someone has come in touch with you, does that mean it's their last life?*

Sadhguru: If you are talking in that context, I have initiated more people that I have not physically met than people that I have actually come in contact with because the number of people I have come in touch with are not too many. People may think it is too many, but it is not too many actually. All the people who come to Inner Engineering,[7] am I their Guru? No. Someone asked me a while ago, "Are only brahmacharis your disciples?" Yes, only they are my disciples. When I say brahmacharis, it is not necessarily only people who got an official initiation. Whether they went through a formal process or not is not the point. In some way, they are on the path. Only brahmacharis are my disciples. If they are not brahmacharis, they are not my disciples anyway. If their interest is something else, where is the question of disciplehood? They cannot be anybody's disciple. Being a disciple is not about someone. You are not this person's disciple or that person's disciple. If you are

---

7   See *Inner Engineering; Emotion: The Juice of Life*, p. 85

a disciple, you are a disciple, that is all. If you are a devotee, you are a devotee. There is no question of you being a devotee of this God or that God – that is just foolishness. You are a devotee and that is all. That is a quality.

There are many who set their eyes upon me but did not take me as their Guru. They may be hanging around here next time around. I may not be here, but they will hang around here because they smelt it, now they want to eat it. "Guru" means "dispeller of darkness." "Gu" means darkness, "Ru" means dispeller. When you say you have a Guru, your darkness is dispelled and why would you be here again? Your darkness is dispelled not because you become light. Your darkness is dispelled because you became nothing, you became darkness yourself, so there is no need to dispel anything. If you stay away from it, it is a terrible thing. If you become it, it is a boundless thing.

Darkness is a terrible thing because you are standing here as a little piece of something. If you become darkness, it is a boundless thing. If I bless you, "May you become boundless," you feel great. If I bless you, "May you become darkness," you think this is a curse. It is not. Darkness is boundless, boundlessness is darkness. Dispeller of darkness does not mean that he will put a light bulb into you. Scholars and teachers tried to put a light bulb into you so that you can see something. A Guru is not trying to put a light bulb into you; he is seeing how to obliterate you. If you found a Guru, that means your darkness is obliterated because you become a part of it. There is no darkness for you; there is only boundlessness for you.

If you have met your Guru, there is no question of being here again. If you smelt your Guru and are still following him, fine. You like the smell, so you are catching up because you did not really meet him as a Guru – you saw him as a man and you liked the smell, but you did not dare to step into him. If you like the smell of roses, wherever the rose is, you go. You could be here just like that. It does not matter because you have not stepped into anything. Don't go on sniffing forever. It is time to step into it and burn because if you don't, you are not using it for the purpose that it is.

If you have an airplane capable of flight but decide to drive it around like a bus, is it wrong? I wouldn't say it is wrong, but it is terrible. To drive an airplane like a car is a terrible and stupid thing to do. Is it wrong to be terrible and stupid? No. Terrible and stupid is bad enough, it need not be wrong. What could take you to a great height, if you use it in a mediocre way, it is just foolish and terrible.

This is not a relationship that endures. If you make this relationship, everything ends. When everything ends, when all things end, a dimension which is not a thing will happen. It is that which this being is longing for, when it is seeking expansion. It is a natural goal. It is just that there is too much diversion on the way. And with every diversion that is taken, people start propounding philosophies as to how this is the right diversion.

Suppose you are travelling somewhere and you found the normal route is obstructed and have to take a diversion – everyone in the car will vote for different diversions and start arguing. Doesn't it happen? Once there is no clear-cut marker, everyone will start making up their own thing, everyone will start claiming this is it. A man who smokes says that this is life, a man who drinks says that this is life, a man who is into some other kind of pleasure says that this is life. A man who takes drugs says that this is life, a man who overeats says that this is life – they are all insisting "this is life." Because of that, diversions happen.

If anything is life, if you do more of it, it should be better. But it does not happen like that. If you eat more, if you drink more, if you smoke more, if you copulate more, life does not get better. People have tried all those things and it has not worked. The only thing that you can do endlessly is doing nothing. And that is the only thing a Guru is, because a Guru is just an empty space. An empty space is the only thing that can dispel darkness, because it *is* darkness – nothing happens there. Where nothing happens, you can make anything happen if you want.

A Guru is just an empty stage. If you enter there, he sets up whatever kind of drama that is necessary for the day, but he is actually an empty stage – four walls with nothing inside. If you step in, you will also become nothing. There is no other way. You looked at him and listened to him, that is not it. You have got to step into him. That is when he is your Guru. Till then he entertains you because he is setting up the appropriate drama for the day.

If you stepped into it, there is no sitting here once again. Such a thing does not arise. If you have not, you only smelt it from a distance, maybe you have taken an addiction for Gurus so you are following them. But if something deeper than the body and the mind happened to you, there is no sitting here again.

Emotion
The Juice of Life

2 BOOKS IN 1

Emotion
The Juice of Life

2
BOOKS
IN 1

SADHGURU

JAICO PUBLISHING HOUSE

Ahmedabad Bangalore Bhopal Chennai
Delhi Hyderabad Kolkata Lucknow Mumbai

Published by Jaico Publishing House
A-2 Jash Chambers, 7-A Sir Phirozshah Mehta Road
Fort, Mumbai - 400 001
jaicopub@jaicobooks.com
www.jaicobooks.com

To be sold only in India, Bangladesh, Bhutan,
Pakistan, Nepal, Sri Lanka and the Maldives.

EMOTION: THE JUICE OF LIFE
ISBN 978-93-86867-50-6

First Jaico Impression: 2018
20th Jaico Impression: 2020

Page design and layout: Inosoft Systems, Delhi

Printed by
Snehesh Printers, Mumbai

Contents

Contents

Introduction

They say elephants can grieve and dogs can laugh, but it is only a human being who is capable of the entire spectrum of emotional response. Depression, malice, bliss, ecstasy, and the many shades in between are uniquely human. We are creatures of emotion. Whether we know it or not, most of us are defined by our joys and sorrows, our love and hate. Our lives can take a complete U-turn, pivoting on just one moment of intense happiness or distress. To be human is to be associated with emotions. And just as well, because emotions are, after all, the juice of life!

It's not just poetic license that allows us to refer to emotions as "juicy." In a literal sense also, emotions are a chemical cocktail that course through our bodies, triggering responses and reactions. The sweet, warm glow of new-found love, the euphoria of intense joy, and the thrill of elation, are an intoxicating mix of chemical stimuli. But while we have no problems with pleasant emotions, unpleasant emotions are the source of much angst in our lives. Emotions like fear and anger release potent chemical brews in our bodies, dominating our thought process and crippling our judgment. Unfortunately, these emotions seem to be their own masters, and their chemical salvos certainly seem to follow someone else's orders. It doesn't take much to set them off. Just one "wrong" word locks us into an endless cycle of unpleasantness.

Our emotions are capable of leaving us stranded in the depths of human experience. But they could also take us to the very heights. Unfortunately, only a miniscule portion of humanity experiences their emotions as a stepping stone. For everyone else, emotions at best bring a little pleasantness, and at worst leave them withered. The question is, are we using our emotions to entangle ourselves or to liberate ourselves?

Turning our emotions into a creative and enriching force is the subject of this book. Sadhguru looks at the gamut of human emotions as he answers various questions posed to him. Despair, joy, bliss, greed, compassion and love find their place here, as he explores the possibilities and pitfalls that each emotion represents. Even profound grief or anger could be turned into a productive force, he explains, if only we make the choice to respond with compassion.

This book turns many conventional beliefs on their heads, such as when Sadhguru tells us that peace of mind is "the 'A' of life, not the 'Z' of life. It is the very beginning." He delves into the chemistry of peace and the reason why most people believe peace of mind is the ultimate aim. As the book progresses, it enters the realm of the mystic – detailing how emotion taken to its ultimate pitch becomes a possibility for liberation. Sadhguru relates some extraordinary stories of a few devotees, whose intensity of emotion crossed the boundaries of logic or understanding.

Perhaps the essence of this book is captured best in Sadhguru's words, "Within you, you have experienced peace and turmoil, joy and misery, ecstasy and agony. So you are capable of all these things. But right now you are conducting this whole experience and chemistry unconsciously. You can also conduct it consciously. That is the whole effort of all spiritual processes."

Isha Publications

Of Madness and Beauty

"Emotion is just the juicier part of the thought."

Though modern societies have done a lot to develop the intellect, emotion is still the most intense experience for most people. Their body, their intellect, and their energies are not so intense, but their emotions – whether anger, hatred, love, compassion or something else – are experientially the most intense.

Thought and emotion are not really different. Thought is dry and logical. Emotion is also rooted in the same logic, but it pretends to be "not logical" to add juice to your life – it is just the juicier part of the thought. Otherwise, your life would be dry and not worth living. Emotion is the deception of nature that encourages you to live, because if you go 100% logically at your life, you would have no reason to live. You would then come to the question, "To be or not to be?" Such questions have come because we have given ourselves too much to logic. We have not given ourselves to the experience of life. Emotion transcends the limitation of simple logic and functions in such a way that it allows you to live. It gives you a reason to go on.

So, thought is dry, and emotion has some juice in it, but they are not different. I don't know why there is so much philosophy about putting the mind and heart together. They are anyway together – they are not separate. Suppose, there is a particular person that you think is wonderful. You would have sweet emotions towards that person. If you think someone else is a terrible person, you would have unpleasant emotions towards that person. You cannot think, "This is a horrible person," and have sweet emotions, and neither can you think, "This is a wonderful person," and have unpleasant emotions. People talk about the conflict between their head and their heart, but there is actually no conflict. It is just that emotions have a certain drag time. They have their own momentum.

Let's say you always thought of someone as a wonderful person. You would have built up so much of emotion, but if that person does something that you do not appreciate, suddenly your logical mind starts saying, "This is a horrible person." But emotion has a drag time. It cannot switch immediately; it has momentum and has to run its course. The mind is clearly telling you that you should have nothing to do with this person, but the emotion is still running its course because it is the last carriage of the train. Thought is the engine. It has passed, but the last carriage takes sometime. So the "emotional you" is also the "thinking you" – the way you think is the way you feel.

Emotions can be a very powerful force of movement if one knows how to gather them, and at the same time, be fluid with them when necessary. If one is incapable of gathering his emotions when needed, then emotions are just pure madness. Once you are overtaken by your emotion, you do not see anything the way it is – everything gets distorted.

Once, a woman who had just lost her husband was seen fanning his grave – a fresh mound of earth.

People who were passing by saw this and were so touched. "How dedicated she is to her dead husband!" They came to her and said, "We know you lost your husband. Your dedication moves us to tears, but please, it is all right. He is dead."

The widow said, "No, I promised my husband that I will not re-marry till the grave is dry."

If you are just emotion, you can be a lot of deception.

Emotions have their beauty; they are the juice of life. At the same time, if you get too soaked in this juice you will lose all your sense. Gautama the Buddha went to the extent of saying that a dry soul is the wisest soul. He is correct. If emotions overpower you, they are nothing short of madness. At the same time, if you have sufficient control over your emotion that you can go into it and come out of it by choice, it is a very wonderful dimension.

"You must go beyond the limitation which is holding you right now."

Questioner: *Emotions seem to be more trouble than they are worth. Aren't we better off without them?*

Sadhguru: If there is no emotion at all in a human being, you cannot call him human. Emotion is a beautiful aspect of human life, without which a human being would become ugly. But as with anything, if emotion becomes unbridled, it becomes madness. If your thought becomes uncontrolled, it will become madness. If your emotion becomes uncontrolled, that too becomes insanity.

People see emotion as a problem because they have painful emotions. If they had beautiful emotions within them, would they call them a problem? If you were full of joy, love and compassion within yourself, if that is how your emotion was taking shape and finding expression, would you consider it a problem? No.

If your body was functioning very well and beautifully, would you call this a problem? No. If it is painful or diseased, then sitting, standing or bending in the morning is really painful – so you would think this body is a problem.

Similarly, you may say you want no emotion simply because you have made a mess out of it. If you had truly beautiful emotions within you which made your life like a flower, you would not think of not having emotions. I am not telling you to leave your emotions or go beyond them. All I am saying is whether it is your body, your mind, your emotion or your energies – the four dimensions which could be in your experience right now – the first and foremost thing is to make them very pleasant. Once they are very pleasant, they are no longer a problem. Only when the emotions are no longer a problem – when people are not aspiring for anything else and are very joyful – does the longing to go beyond arise.

Otherwise all you are trying to do is survive. Even if you are calling for God, it is only a call for survival, isn't it? When you fail to survive here, you are thinking about making it in heaven. If you could not make it here, what is the guarantee that you will make it there? Basavanna, a celebrated sage and a great poet from Karnataka, said, "*Illi salladavaru alliyu sallaraiya*," which means, "Those who do not make it here will not make it there either." So, this is not about going beyond emotion. You must go beyond, but "beyond" does not mean beyond emotion or mind or this or that. You must go beyond the limitation which is holding you right now. Emotion and thought can also become a method and a tool to pave the way for you.

If you use your mind to transcend your limitations, we call this *gnana yoga*. If you use your emotion to transcend limitations, we call this *bhakti yoga*. If you use your body to transcend limitations, we call this *karma yoga*. If you use your energies to transcend limitations, we call this *kriya yoga*. Every one of them is a gateway. A gateway can either block you, or let you beyond. So, your emotions are not to be shunned and rejected to go beyond. You cannot shun them. If you try to become devoid of emotion, you will have suppressed emotions, and you will become dry. Your emotion needs to be accepted in a very deep way so that it becomes your friend. A friend is somebody who is pleasant to you.

2

Paying Attention to the Root

"Whatever you do, you want to experience life in a bigger way than you are experiencing it right now."

Questioner: *Many masterpieces of art depict pain and sadness. I had a conversation with somebody who said he wanted to delve into his misery and paint, because it was only then that he could come up with his deepest emotion. Is there a joy in intense misery also? If you hear some of these melancholic songs for instance, you feel very sad but also, in some way, you are enjoying the song.*

Sadhguru: What they are enjoying is not their misery. Unfortunately, for most human beings on the planet, the deepest experience in their life is pain. There is no depth to their joy, love, or peace. It is all on the surface, and so fragile. Their pain, however, is enduring and deep. Somewhere, every human being wants to know life in a deeper way than he knows it right now. A spiritual seeker is consciously looking for it, but actually, every human being is looking for it.

This is why people take to alcohol and drugs and are mad about sex. This is why people want to jump off the mountains and do absolutely risky things in their life. They are sticking their neck out every day just to experience some butterflies in their stomach. A human being is constantly seeking to experience life deeper, whether he is aware of it or not. For most people, unpleasantness is the deepest experience in their life. They have never known true pleasantness within themselves – it has just been on the surface, it has never really gone deep into their life. That is why people with some intensity, like artists, musicians, painters, and dancers, have always sought pain as an expression. It gives a depth to their work. Joy did not give depth to their work because they do not know how to depict joy in its highest form and deepest possibility. They have never known true joy. They have known pain, so they deepen their pain and try to depict that pain in their work so that there is depth to it. It is unpleasant, but there is depth to it.

Whatever you do, you want to experience life in a bigger way than you are experiencing it right now. You are unconsciously seeking a bigger experience, a bigger slice of life for yourself. Yoga or spirituality brings a method and a science to that longing so that you can put your roots into the absolute core of life. Then, the outside situation will no longer have an impact on you. If this happens, joy is not even the goal of your life anymore; it is just a side effect. It is something that is with you like your breath. It is not something that you are aspiring for, it is not something that you think is a great achievement. It is just there.

When you are already joyful, whatever happens or does not happen is not an issue. You are released from the fruit of action before you start the action. This is not because you developed some dispassion or renunciation about it. It is simply because you are so joyful. Only if you are joyful you can be free from the fruit of action.

∽◈∽

"When people are alive around you, you must value it and give your best every moment of your life."

Questioner: *Sadhguru, how do we deal with the grief that comes from the death of a loved one?*

Sadhguru: I want you to look at this with a certain openness because if somebody is in grief, you don't talk truth to them. You just hug them and comfort them. You tell them pretty lies, you don't speak about truth, isn't it? When they are in grief, they are like little children – they are broken and have become tender. You just handle them tenderly and let them be. Maybe after they get back on their feet, you can tell them the truth, but when they are in grief, it is not appropriate to try and tell them the hard truths of life.

What is grief? First, let's understand that when someone dear to you is lost, your grief is not about a life being lost. You have collaged many things as your life. One important person fell off suddenly, so there is a hole in your life. That is what you are grieving about. You are not grieving because a life has gone from this planet. Every day, thousands of people die, but you are not grieving. You are grieving for this particular one, because it has left a hole, an empty space, in your life, and you are not able to handle that emptiness. So first, let's understand this. The grief is not about somebody dying. The grief is that someone has left your life and gone, and now your life has become crippled in some way.

People grieve the loss of property, the loss of money, the loss of life. In fact, many people grieve loss of money much more than loss of people. They are much more broken by the loss of their money. It is a fact with lots of people. So the question is not about what you lost. The question is how crippled your life has become because of this loss – that is how much you grieve. Let us be straight about this. You are grieving that your life is broken because this person is gone.

I am not trying to belittle your loss or make fun of it. Suppose you had a child. Before the child came, you were fine. The child came and enhanced your life in many ways. Now suppose the child dies. If a life has come into yours, and enriched you in some way, you must live better, but usually you get crippled because you cannot come to terms with this big hole that the loss has created in your life. Instead of enveloping ourselves with the love and joy that we experienced with that life, we are always choosing to make ourselves utterly bitter. I am not saying it is right or wrong. One life is gone, but there is no point crippling another life – either your own or those around you.

Today, life is more secure on this planet than ever before. If you just look back at the previous generations, if your grandmother had five children only two survived. That was normal. Today if you have one, that one survives. It is very rare that it may not survive. Natural selection was happening, and it is happening to all the other creatures. Today because of medical sciences and various other factors, we have stabilized our lives like never before. We should not be complaining any further. We are not wishing it upon ourselves, but if such things happen, we must be able to gracefully cross those situations. Whatever calamities happen to us, we have two options – either we can come out of it broken or we can come out of it stronger. This is the choice we have.

Sometime ago, I met an old lady who was almost 85 years of age. She was from a Jewish family and was a 12-year-old girl during World War II in the year

1939. She was picked up by the Germans along with her brother and parents. The parents were taken away to a separate place, and she never found out where they went. She and her 8-year-old brother were sent to a railway station where they remained for four days. It was winter and was pretty cold. Then the train came, and like cattle, they were all loaded onto it. This little 8-year-old boy got onto the train, but he forgot to take his shoes. So the girl got angry with him and said, "You idiot, wherever you go, I have to take care of you. Can't you get your own shoes?"And those were the last words she said to him, because after that they were sent on separate trains, and she never saw him again. He did not survive. After some six years in the concentration camp, she survived and immigrated into the United States. She told me that on the very day she stepped out of the concentration camp alive, with the rest of her life ahead of her, she made up her mind that she would never again say anything to anybody that she might regret, if that happened to be the last thing that she said to them. That is wisdom. That is strength.

When people are alive, you do all kinds of silly things – you quarrel with them, you fight with them, you say nasty things to them. It is always possible that you may not see them tomorrow. Though we are not wishing it, it is always possible that you and I may die tomorrow, however young and healthy we are. Life is that fragile. When people are alive around you, you must value it and give your best every moment of your life. After they are gone, they are not yours. When they are here, they are yours. When they are here, we should not ignore them. If we cry after they are gone, it is of no use. This may sound brutal, but this is the reality. This is life.

"One can make any emotion into a creative force in one's life."

Questioner: *Sadhguru, you were telling us how one can either come out broken or come out wiser from calamities. Can you elaborate on how sadness can be a means of growth?*

Sadhguru: Most people do not know what it means for misery to strike in the form of life. But for certain people, when it really strikes, everything that they valued in their life is taken away, and a deep sadness settles. There are many ways to handle this sadness. Some people just sit in a corner and drive themselves mad, making everybody miserable. There are others who, when they become sad, find a way of doing some useful work. Usually, it is people who have been hurt like this who become great karma yogis in their lives.

Let me give you an example.

There was a certain person who was a teacher in some primary school in Maharashtra. He lived in a village just off the Sahayadri Mountains with his wife and two children. Then, some dreadful disease took his wife and children, and he was left totally alone. The man was shattered because his whole life was built around those three people. He was on the verge of madness. He simply did not know what to do, so he just walked off into the Sahayadri Mountains and sat there.

He remembered these mountains as they were when he was a child. They used to be green and full of trees. Now, when he was walking in the mountains, it was barren, hot, and unbearable. He sat there for many days, picking fruits and nuts, eating them and just being there. After some time, he decided that only because this mountain had become barren, life had made his life barren. Whether it is true or not is not the point. He decided to do something about this. He lived there like a saint, single-handedly picking up seeds wherever they fell from the trees, and without anybody's support, he planted about four lakh trees and made them grow. He saw them through for twenty-five years. Today, four lakh trees

> are standing on the Sahayadri Mountains because
> of this one man. He is a yogi, though nobody taught
> him any yoga.

One can make any emotion into a creative force in one's life. It is not a negative force. There is no negativity in the existence. We may think something is negative and something else is positive, but a light burns because of negative and positive wires together. Negative is not something to get rid of. It is as important as the positive. If your sadness is reminding you that you are incomplete, it is good. Make use of your sadness to grow. When sadness sets in, if you become more compassionate, more caring, and more loving, you have some sense in you. When you get sad, if you get irritable and angry and think that the whole world is wrong, you are a fool. At that moment, if someone meddles with you, your sadness can very easily become anger. So are you making this sadness into anger or are you making this sadness into love and compassion? It is very easy to become compassionate when you are sad.

Learning to use all your emotions creatively is very important. It is not just happiness which is important. If you have not known sadness, you will not mature. Only if you have known sadness and pain are you a mature person. Otherwise you will never understand what is happening with you, nor will you understand what is happening with anyone else around you.

∿

"Depression means you are unable to maintain the exuberance of life in you."

Questioner: *I see it happening all around us that as we grow older; depression becomes a natural emotion within all of us and takes a toll on human beings. How do we adjust to this situation which is inevitable and happening all the time?*

Sadhguru: Once you declare that depression is a natural process, there is no way out. When you were a child, being joyful was natural to you, not being depressed. So do not declare that depression is natural.

Depression means you are unable to maintain the exuberance of life in you. It happens even in your body. If you are depressed, even the physical body flops. Life within you is not exuberant – it has just gone down and lost its exuberance because you are not doing the right thing with it. You are imposing too much outside nonsense upon the inside. You have not done anything to keep your life energies high.

Depression is a kind of agony. If you have become agony and not ecstasy, it is because a large part of your life energy is happening compulsively, not consciously. It is happening as a reaction to external situations. Once you are happening compulsively, becoming depressed is very normal, because external situations are never a hundred percent in your control.

There are so many things happening in the world that if there is a compulsive reaction within you, getting lost and becoming miserable is natural. If you are not depressed, it must be an accident!

The more exposed you are to life, the more miserable you will become. If you hide yourself in a room, maybe you will be okay as long as the cockroaches cooperate with you, but if they become too many in number, again you become miserable. Whenever people are unable to handle life outside, they try to curtail their life and withdraw. But even that goes out of control, doesn't it? There is one part of you which is constantly seeking expansion – you want to constantly increase the boundaries and areas of your activity. There is another part of you which is getting depressed every time something does not go the way you think it should go. Getting depressed is subject to the non-fulfillment of your expectations.

There is a chemistry to your depression, of course. Every experience has a chemical basis. But if you remain in a certain level of mental alertness and awareness, the chemistry will fall into place by itself. Right now you may not have the capacity to maintain that level of alertness. If the stock market falls today, so many people will get depressed. Many of them may never have even touched that money, but every day they were watching the graphs rising and their mood was in ascendancy. Now they see the graph falling, so their mood is falling. It is just that what they expected to happen, did not happen.

People can cause depression in their mood in so many ways. If you take away what they think is precious, they become depressed. The tragedy with a lot of people, especially in affluent societies, is that they have everything and yet they have nothing. Depression means somewhere, a certain hopelessness has set in. If you go to some very poor village in India, they are really impoverished, but you will still see joyful faces because they have hope – tomorrow is going to be better. In affluent societies that hope is gone. Depression has set in because everything that can be used externally has been fixed. There is food, there is housing, there is clothing, there is everything, but still there is something wrong. They just do not know what. A poor man may simply think, "Tomorrow, if I get a new pair of footwear, everything will be fine." If he gets a new pair of footwear, he will walk like a king with great joy on his face because he has hope – the outside is not yet fixed. In affluent societies, the outside is fixed, but the inside is not, so there is hopelessness and depression. First we must fix the inside, and then work on the outside. Then the world would be beautiful.

What we call as a spiritual process is just this – not just fixing the objective aspect of your life but taking care of the subjectivity of who you are. If that is not taken care of, you will have everything, and you will have nothing.

"As long as you exist here identified as a little body, fear is inevitable."

Questioner: *Where does fear come from?*

Sadhguru: Suppose you were the first person on this planet – which you *are* in your experience. A billion people might have lived on this planet before you, but still, in your experience, everything is new to you. So suppose you are the first person on this planet, and you look up. The sun is shining – you do not know from where. It burns you up. Suddenly, there is a boom and you hear the thunder and rain falls – you do not know from where. Suddenly the wind blows, suddenly a volcano opens up, suddenly the earth shakes one day; you do not know the beginning or the end of this existence. You are this tiny little life in this vast existence. The question, "What will happen to me?" is constantly there, so fear is always right behind the curtains. If you just open it, it will pop up.

As long as you exist here identified as a little body, fear is inevitable. Your physical body is in constant danger, moment to moment. Any moment it may fall apart for some reason. So if you are experiencing your life as a physical body, fear is a natural result of that. Only if your experience of life transcends the limitations of the physical, you can be free of fear.

If your experience of life transcends the limitations of the physical, a dimension beyond the physical becomes a living reality for you. When your inner realities happen consciously, your peacefulness, your joyfulness, your blissfulness are 100% yours. Nobody else or nothing else can ever threaten it. If you make yourself like this, the question of "What will happen to me?" will disappear. Once this question disappears, fear would disappear too.

"Oh, but that looks like such a tall order. Will such a thing happen to me in my life? Do I have to go to the Himalayan caves?" If you are willing to invest just a little bit of time on a daily basis, you can get there. This does not require you to leave your life and go somewhere else. The problem right now is that without making an investment, you are expecting returns.

If you are willing to invest, let us say twenty-five minutes a day, every day, it will pay off. Once this fear is gone, life takes on a completely different dimension. If the fear of "What will happen to me?" exists within you, you will only take half steps, never really full steps. Only when this fear is gone, can you keep the survival instinct down and really look for a bigger possibility in your life. You can truly explore your potential. I am not talking about a teaching or a belief system. I am talking about a technology – a simple way of turning inward and fixing a few things about yourself, so that life takes on a new dimension within yourself.

∽◉∽

"If fear is the basis of what you are doing, it will definitely not bring wellbeing to you."

Questioner: *If fear is such a crippling force, then why is it such an important part of our lives? We have even been told to be God-fearing.*

Sadhguru: Nowadays, it is common for people to say that if you don't go to God's temple, church, mosque or whatever, and give him his weekly "pay-off," he will get angry. He will make your children unhealthy and turn your business upside down. Anybody who has any sense will not want to go anywhere near that sort of man. We have presented the Divine in such a juvenile way.

Do not become a God-fearing person. This is not something that you seek with fear. If fear is the basis of what you are doing, it will definitely not bring wellbeing to you. What you will come to in the end will not be good.

Bhaya (fear) and bhakti (devotion) cannot go together. If you have bhakti in your heart, there is no bhaya in you. If there is bhaya in you, you have not known bhakti in your life. Yet, today, people are talking about bhaya bhakti; the deception has gone so deep! People are not god-loving anymore; they are god-fearing. They fear everything, so naturally they fear God also. You fear just about anything because your identification is limited as a physical entity. Fear is a natural result of this wrong identification.

Till you transcend the limitations of your identity as a physical entity, fear will always be your companion. You may forget about it for certain moments, but if you turn back and see, it is right there. If you start experiencing yourself beyond the limitations of the physical, there is no question of fear.

"Every day, just spend five minutes reminding yourself that you are mortal and you may die today."

Questioner: *I have a phobia – a fear of disease – and I am rather repulsed by diseased and sick people. How do I grow out of this?*

Sadhguru: Nobody wants disease, of course. Nobody would choose to be diseased – everybody wants to be healthy. At the same time, we must understand that once you have a body, illness, old age, and death are natural processes of life. Illness may happen at any moment. We take care to see that we are not ill, but if you become excessively concerned about illness or health, *that* becomes an illness. Just trying to avoid illness is an illness. Illness means something that restricts your life in some way– that is why you do not like it. But the fear of illness also restricts your life. It is an illness by itself.

Especially once you cross forty-five, your fear of illness

becomes much more pronounced. When you were young, you did not think of it because you thought you were immortal. Only after you are forty-five, the fact comes to you. Your fear is not of the illness; your fear is of death. Illness is the passage and the first step towards death. The fundamental fear is always of death. You are still not addressing death directly, you are addressing illness because you know if illness comes, the other one will follow.

Generally, in society, people have been telling you and convincing you that, "After all, fear of death is natural." The problem is that whatever the majority is doing becomes "natural." If the majority was smoking cigarettes, people would say smoking is a natural thing. But a human being is not made to smoke – you are not an automobile! It is not natural for you to smoke, but people will make it natural. So, fear of death has been made natural only by social situations.

Fear of death arises because of a certain sense of ignorance and unawareness. When life happens, the natural process is death. Being afraid of a natural process is unnatural. Fear of death happens simply because you are not in touch with reality. Your identification with this body has become so strong because you have not explored other dimensions. If you had explored other dimensions of experience, the body would not be such a big issue. If you establish yourself in other dimensions of experience, life or death will not make such a big difference. The question of shedding the body is not a big issue. It is a very simple affair.

Once this body has run its course, it will anyway go, whether you like it or not. Whether you approve or disapprove, it will happen. As long as the body is there, taking good care of it is definitely our business. But if you are paranoid about ill health or death, you will not take good care of it. In your anxiety you will destroy the body. The very anxiety of "What may happen to this body?" will destroy it.

People are terrified of just seeing a dead body. Why? People die every day. I am not saying it is a small thing for the people who love and care for them. But why are people afraid to even see a dead body? Living bodies are dangerous – they can do many things to you. Living people are capable of so many things. What will a dead body do to you? The safest thing is a dead body.

When I was about fourteen or fifteen, for about five years, I spent an enormous amount of time in the cemeteries in Mysore. I was somehow drawn to such places. I would sit there the whole night, because everybody was talking about spirits, and I wanted to see them. Then some man told me that every Amavasya (new moon night), he goes and gives his own blood to some ghosts and devils. He showed me his finger all worn out from cutting it and feeding blood. So I went with him and waited the whole night for three Amavasyas, but he would always say, "No. Today, it has not come."

It is good to expose yourself to death. I know you have been told that you should not even utter the word "death" in the house. People have a stupid hope that if you do not utter this word, it will not enter your house. Do you think death will not come to you just because the word "death" is not in your vocabulary?

The process of yoga is completely rooted in death. In fact, you will become spiritual only if you start facing death. If you think of God, you will not become spiritual – you will invent stories. You will seek more survival, wellbeing and prosperity. Thinking of God is not spirituality; it is just another desperate attempt to somehow live well. What is beyond the physical body is what we are referring to as spiritual. Only when you are confronted with death, you start looking beyond this body and the spiritual process will open up for you.

You can use whatever happens around you – illness, death or calamity – to either liberate yourself or entangle yourself. Especially calamities such as death and illness are a tremendous opportunity to look beyond the limitations of what you normally understand as life. You thought the normal understanding of life is getting up in the morning, having a coffee and breakfast, going to work, doing this and that, again eating and doing this and that, throwing yourself around on everybody, and again coming back in the evening. You thought this was life. One day when you are bedridden, suddenly you find life seems to be something very different from what you thought. This need not happen to you if you are intelligent. Everything in this world need not happen to you; you must learn from other people's experiences.

Gautama the Buddha saw just one sick man, one old man, and one dead body, and he realized that any day this could happen to him. So there is no point in running away from it. Let us look at it. If somebody is ill, see that this could have been you – and it could be you any day. The most horrible illness that somebody has – we do not want it nor are we wishing for it – could be yours any day; it does not matter whether you are eighteen or eighty. To face everything with a stable and balanced mind is important. Avoiding it is not the solution. If you avoid it, you only get entangled. Do not avoid illness or death. Please face it.

Several years ago I was in Bangalore, and I went to the vegetable market. The person who was with me was buying vegetables, and I was just walking through the market. Suddenly, I saw this vegetable vendor who was all bright and lit up. I could not believe a man like this was selling vegetables. I looked at him and instantly our eyes locked. I laughed and he also started laughing. I went to him and we started talking.

He had just been a plain vegetable seller when one day, he became ill and thought he was going to die. For over four months he remained so ill that every day he thought, "Today, I am going to die." He went through this for four months, and then he recovered. Then, something wonderful happened to him – he got enlightened!

He said, "Now when anybody who comes to my shop, I bless them to suffer a long illness."

I said, "That's great, but if people come to know, you've had it!"

Every day, just spend five minutes reminding yourself that you are mortal and you may die today. It is possible that today you might fall dead, isn't it? Just remind yourself. Wonderful things will happen to you.

3

From a Horror to a Flower

∽◍∾

"Anger, resentment, hatred—these are all poisons that you drink, and expect somebody else to die. Life doesn't work like that."

Questioner: *In some situations we lose our temper, but it is only later that we realize our stupidity. By then it is too late. How can we control our anger?*

Sadhguru: There is no need to control anger. Right now, are you angry? No. So why should you control something that does not exist? How *can* you control something that does not exist?

Anger is a certain level of unpleasantness, both for you and everyone around you. Most of the time, you suffer more than your victim. And when you get angry, you could do the most idiotic things of your life. It is definitely not an intelligent way to exist.

Being angry about something or the other comes from a strong sense of likes and dislikes. This comes from a very deep identification with a certain way of thinking and feeling, which according to you, is the best way to live, think and feel. When someone is not in line with that, you get angry with them. As your likes and dislikes and your identifications become stronger with something or the other, all that you are doing is excluding the existence. If you say, "I like this very much," you are excluding the rest of the existence in a big way at that moment. The stronger the like or dislike becomes, the deeper the exclusion becomes. Anger overflows because you have not included someone or something as a part of yourself. The very process of liberation is to include, not exclude. In inclusion, you become liberated. The day when everything – the whole existence – is included in you, you are liberated. In exclusion you become trapped, you become separate.

You do not wish to be angry, of course, but it is happening because you are ascribing an outside source for what is happening within you – and that is not true. Just see that anger is something that you are creating. Why are you creating something that you do not want? There is only one basic cause – you are ignorant of yourself.

If you knew how your system functions and how to manage this system, why would you create anger? Anger is not only damaging the external situation, it is also damaging the internal situation. People are causing enormous amounts of anger within and creating health problems for themselves. Accordingly, consequences will happen for external situations.

For every action that you perform, there is a consequence. You cannot avoid the consequence. When you cannot avoid the consequence, action should be controlled. They can be controlled only if a human being is controlled within himself or herself. When one is in perfect balance, only then will one perform harmonious action. Still, there are always consequences. There are enough consequences in the life process as it is – you do not have to go about creating new consequences for yourself.

Especially if situations around you are rotten, is it not very important that you keep yourself in the most pleasant possible manner and see how to spread this pleasantness around you? If your actions were coming from your intelligence, this is how you would act. If situations around you are hopeless, it is all the more important that you keep yourself as beautiful as possible and see how to make the situation happen the way you want. Whatever you are, that is what you will spread around you. If you are angry, you will spread anger. With anger, more unpleasantness will come into the situations around you.

Anger is enormous intensity. Intensity is the only thing that man is seeking. The reason why all the thrillers, action movies, and sports events are so popular is because people want some intensity, somewhere. The only way they know how to be intense is either through physical action, or through anger, or through pain. The very reason why drugs and sex have become such big things in the world is because somehow, people want to experience some intensity at least for a few moments. Intensity releases you from many things. Anger could also release you from many things, but the problem with anger is, it is not pure intensity within you; it gets entangled with the situations around.

It is not necessary that only your anger should propel you into action. The most intense experience you have had in your life is probably anger. That is the reason why you are sanctifying anger, because it propels you into action. Unfortunately, you have never known the intensity of joy or love. But love and compassion can also propel you into action – very gently, but very wonderfully and effectively. At work and at home, would you like to live with angry people, or peaceful and joyful people? Obviously you would want to live with peaceful and joyous people. Please remember, everyone around you is expecting the same thing. Every human being around you is always expecting to live and work with people who are peaceful and joyful.

"If you use the horror of who you are as manure, the beauty of who you could be could flower."

Questioner: *How do I free myself from the jealousy that arises within me?*

Sadhguru: As long as you feel you are insufficient the way you are, the moment you see someone whom you think has more than you, you feel jealous. Instead of trying to battle jealousy, it is better to work towards your fulfillment. When you are very joyful, are you jealous? No. Only when you are unhappy, you are jealous. Do not worry about jealousy. If every moment of your life, your energies are bubbling with ecstasy, how will there be jealousy? Such things do not exist. Do not try to work with that which does not exist; you will get lost. What exists right now is your happiness and unhappiness – the rest is all an offshoot of that. The root of your jealousy, envy and all these problems is that you are unhappy.

Freedom will not happen by giving up anything because what is there to give up? Right now, there is no jealousy in you. Jealousy is not a part of your nature. Now and then you create it. If you had created it because you wanted it, then it is okay – it is your joy. If you are happy in anger, fear and jealousy, create them. But that is not so, they are not happy experiences for you. So, why have you created them? You create them because you do not have the necessary awareness within yourself.

If you give up something forcibly, it will return to you in some other way. So many distortions of human personality have happened in society today, simply because we are trying to do something with ourselves forcibly, without understanding our nature.

If you really want to be free, what should you do? First and foremost, you should understand where your bondage is – what you are identified with. The moment you are identified, you are in confrontation with existence. The whole spiritual process is to dis-identify you, so that you are no longer in conflict with existence. You are just experiencing everything the way it is, not trying to label it this way or that way, or trying to make a divine or devil out of it.

If you use the horror of who you are as manure, the beauty of who you could be, could flower. What is this "horror," and what does it mean? When you find a person horribly prejudiced and jealous, angry, hateful and fearful, that is the horror of what a human being can be. Existentially, in the physical world around you, isn't it true that anything that produces the best flowers and fruits is always the most horrible thing? These days people talk a lot about organic vegetables. What it means is that you like vegetables nourished by shit, not by fertilizer coming from a bag!Somewhere, you understand that this is what produces the best kind of flowers, fruits or vegetables – it is the best manure.

This is the logic of life. This is something you need to understand, as symbolism and a psychological tool, and also spiritually. The simple logic of your mind says that if you want to produce good flowers in the garden, put a lot of flowers into the soil, and more beautiful flowers will come out of it. That is not how existence works. That is logical, but existence is not logical. The soil demands stinking waste, not fragrant flowers. Stinking filth is not just *okay*, that is what the soil *demands*. If you put it to the root, wonderfully fragrant flowers will come out of it. This is the way the existence is working.

All these horrors which make *you* into a horror – your anger, hatred, jealousy, prejudices – please see with how much intensity they happen within you. If only meditation happened with that much intensity, wouldn't it be wonderful? Wouldn't you be going places? Definitely you would.

All the things which make a human being into a horror travel on the basic vehicle of intensity. If your anger, fear or jealousy were weak, it would not mean anything. When they burn within you, that is when they are something. And they always burn within you with great intensity. So, one element of spirituality is there with you, the only question is to learn how to make use of it. If you use the filth and apply it to the root, it is good. If you smear it on your face, it is not good. If you do not have this awareness, you will try to apply fragrance to the roots and may kill the plant. You need to apply filth, not fragrance. That is how the whole world works, and that is how you should also work.

Do not try to work on the byproducts. You feel you are not sufficient simply because you are not well within yourself. Anybody who is not feeling blissful is actually ill. Maybe you are in a state of socially accepted wellbeing – because the majority of people are with you, and this is a democracy – but you are ill in terms of life. Unhappiness has come to you because you are not in tune with your own nature. No attempt has been made to look at yourself carefully and understand that the seat of your experience is within you. If the seat of your experience is within you, and you have to decide and manage how well you live here, the first thing is to turn inward and look at the nature of who you are.

If that does not happen, your wellbeing is accidental. When your wellbeing is accidental, jealousy, hatred, and insecurity are a natural part of your life. It is like we are burning something and there is smoke. Do not battle with the smoke. You have to battle with the fire.

"If you sit here as just a piece of life, you will be in perfect harmony with every other life."

Questioner: *Sadhguru, the feeling of hatred and greed are very strong and dominant in us. Why is it that we have become like this?*

Sadhguru: Once we hold somebody else as the source of who we are or what we are right now, invariably, people around you will fail you in so many different ways. No human being is going to function hundred percent the way you want them to. The bigger your expectations, the more failure you will see with people around you. When they fail you, and things do not happen the way you think they should happen, you truly believe *they* are the cause for your misery. So naturally, anger arises. When this anger gets organized, it becomes hatred. The very moment you think that the source of who you are, or the basis of your experience in this life is somebody else, you have started the game.

Maybe initially it started in a pleasant way, "Oh, I am so happy because of you." This game is going to turn sour in no time because the same person who did certain things and made you happy today is going to do certain things tomorrow that he or she wants, which is going to make you very unhappy. No human being can live up to your expectations. Not one human being on the planet will be exactly the way you expect him or her to be. Once this happens, you think someone else is the source of your misery and naturally anger and hatred will follow.

If you sit here as just a piece of life, you will be in perfect harmony with every other life. That is a reality. It is not my idea or your idea; that is the way existence is. But you cooked up a separation. "I hate these people because they are not doing things my way. My ideals are the greatest ideals and these people do not have such ideals. These are fallen people so I can hate them." You are cooking up an ideal. You are trying to cover one lie with another lie. It is not a solution; it is only complicating the problem. At least if you see, "I just hate these people," and if you live in hatred for three days, slowly you will wonder, "Why am I like this?" Because that is your humanity. But if you back it up with your ideals and ethics, you can continue to hate them for the rest of your life.

Greed is a very relative term. One person thinks living in a palace is a necessity. Another person thinks it is greed. This happened some time ago – I met a swami who lived under a tree. He had made it his life's mission to constantly deride all those other swamis who had built some simple shelters for themselves. He spent his lifetime saying how these people were lost, how these people were corrupted and how they had given themselves to comfort and luxury – because he himself lived under the tree, braving all the rigors of the weather. He would say, "They are pompous, look at the way they have decorated their huts." They just wanted to make the hut a little beautiful, so somebody put a flower garden, a couple of flower plants in front of their house; somebody else painted it a little bit – but he thought all that was pompous. I had to remind him that thinking that you are better than everybody else is the most pompous, stupid thing you can do.

So what greed is, is very relative. You are never greedy, but somebody else who has gotten to a place where you are aspiring to get, is greedy in your eyes. You are trying to make a million bucks – you have not made it – but you think the man who *has* made it is greedy. If you make it, one million bucks is not greedy; ten million is greedy because somebody else has gone there. This need to accumulate is so strong because there is a certain sense of insufficiency. Who you are is not enough; you want to be something more than what you are right now. The moment you reach there, you want to be something more than that.

I want you to know this: even if we hand over the whole planet to you, you will still look up at the stars because there is something within you which is constantly seeking expansion. However much you give it, it is not going to settle. Give it the whole galaxy, it will still look for more galaxies. There is something within you which is seeking boundless expansion. So, greed, as you know it in the world today, has happened because your inner nature wants to find boundless expansion, but you are trying to satisfy this thirst for boundlessness through physical means. That is the basis of your greed.

There is nothing wrong with your greed; it is actually a spiritual process. Meditation is just this – a powerful desire without a goal. If your desire and your energy become full force, but not towards anything in particular, this is meditation.

Questioner: *I would like to know how to handle guilt. And another aspect of my life that I have has struggled with is, how* *to live in the moment with joy. I have made an effort to avoid living in the past or the future but even the present is not easy or peaceful. It is overshadowed by actions of the past, and I have not been very successful in not fearing what the future holds.*

Sadhguru: Fear is a natural emotion in a human being, but guilt is socially cultivated. People feel guilty about different kinds of things in different societies. What a person from India may feel guilty about, an American will do without any sense of guilt. For something that an Indian does without any sense of guilt, an American may suffer guilt. So, guilt is a socially cultivated emotion. It is not a natural thing. We are going through all this simply because we have labeled something as good and something as bad. Anyway, you are only guilty of what you did yesterday, not what you are right now.

Nothing happens out of guilt except damage to ourselves – it is focused towards you. The worst guilt that you must suffer from is that you are not living joyfully. Causing suffering to yourself is the worst guilt because if I try to cause suffering to you, you have some defense against it. But if you start causing suffering to yourself, this being is a totally helpless being. So, the worst guilt that you suffer from is, you are torturing an absolutely defenseless being, which is yourself.

How can you live joyfully? You don't have to do anything. If you stop messing around with your mind and stupid ideas about life, then it is natural for life to be joyful. So, forget all this nonsense about living in the moment because anyway where else can you live? You only live in the moment.

One thing that is being thrown around all over the place is, "Be in the moment." This looks like a great teaching, but my question is, "Can anybody be anywhere else other than this moment?" Whatever you do, anyway you are in this moment. But people say, "No, we are not in the moment; we are thinking about this and that." So, what this "teaching" is essentially saying is – "You should not think." It took millions of years to develop this brain and now the teaching is "Do not think!" Whether you are thinking about yesterday or a million years later, you are still in this moment. This teaching looks like a great teaching because for most people, their thought is an unpleasant experience. If your thought is a wonderful experience for you, you would not take this teaching from anybody.

This has become a malaise, particularly in the West, and it has caught on in the Indian cities because the Indian urban population is more Western than the West. They are a little more American than American.

This happened – two young women met in a restaurant. One said to the other, "I intend to not marry till I am thirty."

The other said, "I intend to not be thirty as I am already married."

If something is said, you can call it a teaching only if there is a possibility that someone could get there. If no one can get there, that is called rubbish.

"The moment you say something is wrong, you cannot avoid it. The moment you try to avoid it, that will fill your mind."

Questioner: *If we become egoless and humble, can we be free from suffering?*

Sadhguru: Everybody is claiming to be egoless and humble. Claiming to be humble is the worst sort of ego. One who claims to be egoless is a horror of an ego. At least a straightforward ego is good.

What is an ego? Any number of people are claiming to be egoless and the victims of other people's ego. If there is no ego, there is no survival process in a human being. So the question of somebody being egoistic and somebody not being egoistic does not arise. Nobody can escape this; once you are identified with your physical body, the ego is there. Is it good or bad? It is neither good nor bad once you realize that you can create your ego the way the external situation demands. To operate in different kinds of situations, you need different kinds of egos. But the problem is that you have lost the distinction between what is you and what is your ego.

When there is no distinction, you start functioning in foolish ways which cause pain and suffering to yourself. And whenever you are capable of causing pain and suffering to yourself, invariably you will also share it. It cannot be helped. People think, "It does not matter that I suffer, but I want everybody to be happy." Such things do not work. If you do not know what it means to be joyful, you cannot make anybody joyful.

These miserable people who claim to be egoless think they are living for everybody else, but nobody wants them to live because good intentions alone do not make anything good. It is the way you are, which makes the difference in the world. You don't need any good intentions. If you keep your humanity up, alive and active, why do you need good intentions? If you put your humanity to sleep, then you need good intentions, morals and ethics. If your humanity is alive, everything will happen the way it needs to happen from within you.

The moment you say "spirituality," the first thing that the so-called spiritual people tell you is that you must give up the common ego and pick up a spiritual ego – which is very dangerous. Whenever your ego is supported by a scripture or a God, it is the most horrible kind of ego.

Those people who claimed to be doing God's work, always did the maximum amount of damage on this planet. Human nature is such that if you do something stupid today, tonight your intelligence will bother you. Everybody thinks they need to do God's work. If God is almighty, do you have to do his work? No. You just mind your business. But too many people are doing God's work on the planet, and that is the biggest ego, but it gets so well-polished and smooth that nobody can catch it. It is so slippery.

People have always been trying to divide the material and the spiritual as two different parts. This division has caused so much confusion and allergy towards spirituality, because today, in most people's minds if you live badly, dress badly and eat badly, then you must be spiritual. That has been the idea for a long time. That is why nobody wants to go spiritual.

The physical by itself has no purpose of its own. Your body is very important. You have to feed it, clothe it, decorate it, and pamper it in so many ways. Suppose tomorrow morning, that *something* which is within – which you never experienced – slips away, nobody would want to deal with this body. The physicality is like the peel of the fruit. The moment you eat the fruit, the peel goes straight to the trash can. The peel is valuable only because it contains the fruit. Once the fruit is gone, the peel does not mean anything.

If you were just eating the peel of the fruit, how would life be? It should have been bitter. If life was continuously bitter, all of you would be enlightened by now. The problem is that peel has imbibed a few spots of sweetness, because of its association with the fruit. What you call as life is just trying to extract juice out of those few spots of sweetness, without understanding that this sweetness has entered the peel only because of its association with the fruit, not otherwise.

If you put a drop of honey here on the floor and keep the honey jar out there, even a little ant, which has one millionth of your brain, has enough intelligence to know that it must go for the jar. Nature trusted your intelligence and thought that if it puts a drop of sweetness into your physicality, you would naturally go for that which is beyond the physical because you would understand that is where it comes from. Yet today people are trying to disprove nature's trust, simply because they have become identified with the simple egos that they have taken on. You are proud of the kind of nose you have or the kind of qualifications you have or the kind of home you live in. They have become the basis of one's life. And because of this, the simple awareness that whatever little sweetness you taste in the peel could be multiplied a million fold if you go for the fruit, is not happening to humanity.

The reason you identify yourself with your clothes, homes, or something else, is because nothing else worthwhile has been found within yourself. You have to cling to something to make yourself into something of worth. Otherwise, there is no purpose to live on. It is just that people are constantly looking outward. They have never turned inward and looked at the nature of what this is. They have to hang on to many things to make themselves complete. But such a thing has not happened, has it?

Right now you have identified yourself, but essentially, you are just a piece of life who is *on* for a limited amount of time, isn't it so? And this piece of life is complete. It does not need any additions to make it good. This is just fine by itself.

"Your wanting to possess something is essentially coming from a certain sense of unfulfilled experience of life."

Questioner: *How is it possible to live without getting possessive and attached?*

Sadhguru: Why do you want to possess somebody or something? It is your way of including something as a part of yourself. Yoga means to become all-inclusive. Your possessiveness is also yoga, but it is a very stupid and painful yoga. And it will always remain incomplete and frustrating, because you are never going to possess everything; there will always be much that remains out of your possession. It will never reach its goal. So you have to learn to include everything as a part of yourself, without the need to possess.

To enjoy something, does somebody have to write on a paper that it belongs to you and it is only yours? That is what you are asking in life. To enjoy anything, it must be yours. Even to enjoy a child, he has to be yours. Somebody has to check your DNA and say it has come from your body, not from somebody else's body. You cannot enjoy anything the way it is. The only little pleasure that you have in your life is that something belongs to you. And if even what belongs to you belongs to everybody, you cannot enjoy it. This is a perversion and a disease. You can enjoy it only when it belongs to you and only you. Or your enjoyment is that nobody else has what you have. That is definitely sickness.

Unfortunately, 95% of the population is psychologically ill. If they wear some clothes, nobody else should be wearing those clothes; only then can they enjoy it. If everybody is wearing it, they cannot enjoy it. If they build a house, nobody else should have that kind of house. Only then they can enjoy it. Anything and everything is like this. This is not joy; this is just illness.

Now, if I tell you "do not possess," you are not going to stop anyway because this is a very deep-rooted problem. This is not going to go away because of somebody's advice. You may shift your objects of possession from this to that, but the longing or the need to possess is not gone. All you are trying to do is somehow find fulfillment, because you are unable to bear the incompleteness of who you are. Try hard – it will not get you anywhere.

If you realize it is not getting you anywhere, you must be sensible enough to shift. Try something; if it works, go on that path. If it does not work, leave that and try something else. You will see, none of these things will work. All of them will create a sense that they may work, but they will deceive you later. Don't try in a lukewarm way; try *absolutely*. If you try absolutely, within 24 hours you will know. If you try off and on in lukewarm ways, it will take a lifetime to know. Whatever your problem is, go all the way into it. Within 24 hours you will see that this is no good and that it will never work. It will be hundred percent clear to you. Once it is clear to you, you will definitely shift. Your intelligence will flower.

The only thing that can be trusted is intelligence because life is intelligence. A tree blossoms, it is a certain intelligence. The very earth that you walk upon is intelligent, the air that you breathe is intelligent. One way of looking at life is, it is just an explosion of intelligence. What you call as creation and what you refer to as the Creator is the ultimate intelligence. That is the only thing you can trust right now, and that will function only if you go all the way.

It will only happen when you as a piece of life are alive to the core. Only when you have touched that, you will find everything is fine. Now you can play life like a football game. You are on when it is on, when you want to switch it off it is off. Then, nothing is a problem.

"You become free not by excluding yourself; you become free only by including everything as a part of yourself."

Questioner: *Sadhguru, how do I not get attached to somebody or something when they have become everything to me?*

Sadhguru: If you have become so attached, why are you still there? Go a little more strongly into your attachment till nothing of you remains. If you try to detach yourself, you will only damage yourself because the very fact that you are attached right now means that attachment is your way. If you try to go against it, you will only hurt yourself. If attachment is your way, get totally attached. If you take two substances and attach them together, if the attachment is total or complete, you cannot differentiate one from the other. Only if the attachment is not total, you can see the two parts separately. Once you cannot tell the difference, there is no problem.

This question arises because somebody, somewhere, told you that "attachment is bad, don't get attached to anything." This question arises because of a misunderstanding. It could also be arising because of the pain that attachment creates. But if the attachment is total, the pain will go away, and if you don't have these old teachings within you, there is really no problem. Get so totally attached that you cannot make out the difference.

When you cannot tell the difference, there will be absolutely no problem about it.

If you get attached to your being, what you call as "myself" will not exist. Attachment is a problem only when you get attached to your own body, your ideas, emotions, philosophies, your own rights and wrongs, and likes and dislikes. If you can truly get attached to another being, it is wonderful. But when you get attached to your own body, thoughts, and emotions, you become so limited. When you get attached to your own likes and dislikes, you become even more limited.

So get attached. Why are you hesitating? If you are getting attached to *your* idea of what the other person is, then it is trouble. The pain of attachment is only because you are getting attached to your idea of what the other person is, not really to another being. If you can enjoin your energies with another person's, it is just fantastic, and there is really no problem. That is what attachment means. Deepen your attachment so absolutely, become so attached that time and space cannot separate you. Right now, you hesitate to be attached because of these teachings that attachment is bad, so time and space is a problem.

If you are going to just sit with anybody as a limited person, with your likes and dislikes, you will hesitate to be attached. Your personality is only a bundle of likes and dislikes, and cravings and aversions within you. This is the fundamental basis, or building blocks of your personality. Yet, existing in the world with likes and dislikes is a very foolish way to exist. Please look at it carefully: the fundamental basis of your bondage is in likes and dislikes. Unfortunately, the logical mind makes you believe that doing what you like is your freedom. While operating on the physical realm itself, even with your work or family, likes and dislikes make you do stupid things. If you don't like somebody, even if this person is doing something wonderful, you will not see it. If you like somebody, even if they are doing terrible things, you cannot see it anymore. The moment you get trapped in likes and dislikes, you lose your discretion, and your intelligence is forsaken. You cannot function as per what is needed at that moment. Awareness is simply impossible once you get trapped in likes and dislikes.

Yoga means attachment. When you get attached to the existence, you are yoga. People have misunderstood "non-attachment" so badly. You become free not by excluding yourself; you become free only by including everything as a part of yourself. Freedom will not come because you make yourself exclusive. If you detach yourself from everything, you will become exclusive in the existence; you become more and more of an entity. If you include everything as a part of yourself, you will have no identity left. So become attached totally. Don't be stingy in your attachment.

4

Break the Barriers

∼☙∽

"To be peaceful is the fundamental of your life."

Questioner: *We often have to deal with chaotic situations. How do we remain peaceful in such situations?*

Sadhguru: All of us need peace in our lives. You wish to be in peace, but the mind is agitated, so mentally you have no peace. Suppose you lose your peace, naturally, first you will have a quarrel with your husband or wife. As it progresses, you go and yell at your neighbor. As it progresses further, you yell at your boss. The day you yell at your boss, everyone knows that you need medical help. Yelling at your husband, wife or neighbor may be perceived as normal because everyone is doing that. Yelling at your boss would be taking it too far. Now you are in a situation where you have to go to a doctor. He gives you a tablet. Once the tablet goes into your system, you become peaceful – at least for a few hours. When some chemical is put into the system, at the level of the body and mind, agitation leaves and a little peace sets in. So, peace is a sort of chemistry within the body. Similarly, every emotion has a type of chemistry. Whatever the feeling is, it will have a corresponding chemical system within the body that will adjust with it. If we are peaceful, a peaceful chemistry is there within us. Or, if we can create that kind of chemistry within us, automatically peace is there within us. In yoga, we approach it both ways.

With the right kind of practices, we can bring about a change in our internal chemistry and bring it to a particular level, so that whatever be the situation, we will always be in peace. Right now your peace is a slave to the external situation. If the situation is conducive to you, you remain in peace. If the situation is not okay for you, there is a problem. Only when your peace is not enslaved to the external situation, and your inner self remains the same no matter what the external situation is, then we can call it yoga. In other words, you can say that yoga is the science of creating the right kind of chemistry.

If you have the right kind of chemistry, being peaceful and joyful is the only way – it cannot be any other way. To be peaceful and joyful is not the end of life; it is the beginning of life. If you are not even peaceful, if you are caught up in your mental nonsense, you have not started living yet. Being peaceful or joyful is the most basic requirement. Even if you want to enjoy your breakfast or dinner, you must be peaceful. If you are agitated, can you enjoy your dinner? No. Being peaceful is the very beginning. But today, people go about propagating that the highest dimension of one's life is to have peace of mind.

Unfortunately, because large populations of the world have not made this beginning, there are people propagating it as if it was the ultimate in life. It is so unfortunate that the so-called spiritual people are going about telling people that to be peaceful is the ultimate. To be peaceful is the most fundamental thing. This is not enlightenment or God. This is the "A" of life, not the "Z" of life. It is the very beginning.

"When you are happy by your own nature, not because of somebody else or something else, you have enormous freedom in your activity."

Questioner: *If it is so fundamental, why do peace and happiness seem to be elusive for most people?*

Sadhguru: When it is such a basic requirement, why is happiness so elusive? Why is it that so many people do not even know how to sit peacefully in one place? The basic reason is that somewhere, we believe that by fixing the outside, everything will be okay with life. India still needs a lot of fixing on the outside, but there are many western societies where they have fixed the outside sufficiently. An enormous amount of human activity has happened. Because of science and technology, we have done so many things that the very face of the planet has changed. The way the planet used to look has completely changed in one hundred years. So much fixing has happened that the planet's life is under threat. We have fixed the world to that extent. In spite of that, have people become peaceful and happy?

The external sciences can bring you comforts and conveniences. Today, in terms of comforts and conveniences, ordinary citizens in the world have what royalty did not have a hundred years ago. In spite of that, it cannot be said that humanity is any more peaceful or loving than what it was a hundred years ago.

Right now, in many ways, people's happiness, peace and love are mortgaged to the external situation. They are never going to be happy or truly peaceful because no matter what kind of a person you are, however powerful you are, even if you are superhuman, you do not have absolute control over the external situation. Even with two people in the family, you do not have total control over the situation.

You can manage the external situation only to a certain extent, whereas your interiority can be taken into absolute control. As there is a science for external wellbeing, there is also a science for inner wellbeing which has not been looked at for a very long time. This is offered as a technology, so it is just a question of the intensity you practice it with – it works accordingly.

Every human being is capable of existing here in blissfulness. One of the things that people who practice yoga always hear from their relatives and friends is, "Why can't you take that smile off your face?" Suddenly, you seem to be joyful all the time, by yourself, not because of anything that is happening with your life. You are simply joyful, because that is your nature. When you were a child, you were like this to some extent. You were simply happy. Even if there was a death in the family, you were still happy. Only after you became a certain amount of mind, then you started suffering everything. For most people, nothing has gone wrong with their lives, but they fear it may go wrong. If you are using an external stimulus, it is a problem. You should find an inner stimulus.

What we are saying in terms of yoga is just this. This is a technology of finding an inner stimulus to all the inner dimensions of who you are. You have an inner stimulus for your joy, your bliss, your peace, and your love; now you do not depend on anybody. You are always peaceful, joyful, and loving. When you are happy, you are happy by your own nature, not because of somebody else or something else. Now, you have enormous freedom in your activity. Even if the whole world does not agree with you, it does not matter – you still know what to do. Only when you are happy by your own nature, you are not a vested interest in this world. Otherwise, wherever you go, you are trying to extract happiness from situations and people around you. For many people, their friends gradually turn into their enemies because they are trying to extract happiness out of their friends, and their friends are trying to extract happiness out of them. This is bound to lead to a war.

If your life is about expressing your happiness, not extracting happiness, you will be very different. Just look at the experience of your life. The moments when you are expressing your happiness are the most beautiful moments in your life. In expressing your happiness maybe you smiled, or gave somebody a gift, or just hugged somebody. Yet, these things have been a bigger and more beautiful experience within you than pursuing happiness and doing big things. Do you know how sweet life becomes when your whole life is an expression of your happiness?

"When you live here as a potential calamity, being joyful is very difficult."

Questioner: *Sitting here in the ashram and listening to this discourse is beautiful, but when we have to go back to the noisy, hectic city, it's different. We can't just detach ourselves from situations and come here. So what do we do?*

Sadhguru: We are not talking about detachment, nor is it necessary to come to the ashram. We definitely seek a conducive atmosphere, but that is not the hundred percent of it.

Do you see that everything that a person does seems to be happening in the pursuit of happiness? Fundamentally, why do you do all the things that you are doing? For example, why did you start a family? Somewhere, you believed that it would bring you happiness. Probably for some, they got married because of family pressure, but why did you give in to the pressure? Because somewhere you thought making them happy was your happiness. You picked up people, you picked up education, you picked up your profession, you picked up so many things on the way only because you believe these are all instruments to make you happy. You educate yourself, you pursue careers, you run businesses, you raise families, you run the rat race. Why? Somewhere you believe that if all these things happen, you will be happy. At every point you believe, "If I get that job I will be happy, if I get that promotion I will be happy, if I get married I will be happy, if I have a child I will be happy." At every point you believed, "If these things happen, I will be happy." So you are doing all these things in pursuit of happiness.

Either you go at it straight or you go about it roundabout, but still you are in pursuit of happiness. Either you route it through heaven, your wife or husband, the bottle, or something else, or you just approach it directly.

If happiness is your objective, let us look at the very

fundamentals of it. Whenever you were happy, happiness did not rain upon you from outside; it found expression from within. Maybe an external stimulus was there, but you were happy inside. You were never happy somewhere else. Something happened that ignited this happiness within you, but the experience of happiness was always within you. Happiness is within, but the key is outside.

There are many ways to understand this. One simple way is that although you may be identified with many things in your life, in this moment when you sit here, you are just a certain amount of life energy. You may be a doctor, you may be a policeman, you may be a housewife, you may be many things socially, but this moment, existentially you are just a certain amount of life energy. You are just a piece of life. This life energy may be listening or speaking or doing something else, but beyond your identification, if you simply look at your experience, you are just a certain amount of energy functioning in a certain way.

This life energy, which you right now call as "myself," sometimes has been very joyful, sometimes utterly miserable, sometimes very peaceful, sometimes in turmoil, sometimes in agony, and sometimes ecstatic. This life energy is capable of all those things. If you are given a choice, to be either miserable or blissful, what would you choose? You would obviously choose to be blissful. Everybody has that much intelligence. Nobody has to write a Veda or an Upanishad to tell you, "Please choose bliss. Do not choose misery." The very life in you is longing to be joyful and blissful. There is no other choice.

In spite of this, so much misery has happened simply because your life energies are functioning compulsively. They are not functioning consciously anymore. They are functioning as a reaction to the situations in which you live. If your inner experience is decided by what is happening outside of you, then your very way of being is bound to be accidental. If you exist here as an accident, you are always a potential calamity. When you live here as a potential calamity, being joyful is very difficult. That is all that has happened right now.

One day, a shriveled old man was sitting in a "Bachelors Only" club in the mid-morning, drinking whisky after whisky and chain-smoking. A woman observed this and went up to him and asked, "Hey, old boy. How come you are drinking and smoking away like this in the morning? It looks like you don't have a care in the world."

He said, "Yes, I don't have a care in the world."

The woman asked him, "What is the secret of your life? How come you are here like this?"

The old man replied, "The secret of my life is, I have my fifth whisky by noon, I chain-smoke through the

day, and I eat just whatever I please. This is the
secret of my life."

She said, "That's amazing. How do you manage
this? Anyway, how old are you?"

He said, "I'm 22."

Different people have different ideas of wellbeing, but
fundamentally, you really feel well when you are happy. When
you are happy, even if you are physically ill, you still feel well.
Or in other words, what you call as human wellbeing is being
peaceful and joyful. But somewhere, you have missed the
fundamentals of life; you did not grasp the basics. That is why,
even though happiness is so important and fundamental, it
seems to be so elusive for most people.

"If you are joyful, no exploitation can ever touch you."

Questioner: *Can a joyful person be exploited or bullied?*

Sadhguru: Whichever way you are – joyful or miserable – you
could be exploited by somebody. It is not because you are joyful
or miserable that somebody can exploit you. If somebody gets

into a position of advantage, either because of his capability or because of the social situation or something else, he could exploit you. That is a possibility in the world wherever you go. But if you are anyway joyful, exploitation has no impact on you.

Exploitation can happen in many ways, but misery is an exploitation by itself. Somebody else exploiting you is one thing, but you are exploiting your own life, causing misery to yourself. But if you are a joyful person, nobody can truly exploit you because exploitation means doing something against your wellbeing. When you are a joyful person, who can do anything against your wellbeing? Even if they put you to death, you will die joyfully. Nobody can exploit a person who is truly joyous. No matter what is being done to him, he has got nothing to lose. If he is killed, one joyful being is lost. He lost nothing, he just lost a body, it does not mean anything to him – at least the pains and the struggles of the body are over for him.

Only a miserable person is constantly thinking about somebody exploiting him. Every little action, they think there must be some undercurrent of something else. You may have seen this happening. As people become more miserable, they are constantly afraid that somebody will exploit them. All the time, they are paranoid that somebody will take advantage of them. What is there to take advantage of in most people? They have made themselves into such a disadvantage that whichever way they exist, they are at a disadvantage. Is that not exploitation?

If you are miserable, nobody needs to exploit you, everything is exploitation. If you are joyful, it does not matter what they do, no exploitation can ever touch you. If they do something stupid to you, they are only demeaning their life, not yours. You can make a miserable person's life meaningless. How can you make a joyful person's life meaningless? His existence is beautiful by itself. He is not looking for any meaning. Exploitation is possible on the planet only because a large number of people are miserable. Otherwise, there is no exploitation.

For example, if you look at the crucifixion of Jesus... physically it is the most horrible thing that can happen to a human being. When somebody is driving nails into your hands and legs, when such physical pain happens, you should scream, yell, and curse the world. But it seems he said, "They know not what they are doing. Forgive them." Can a man say this if he is suffering or if he is in misery? He could say this only because he had an inner source of joy which could not be touched even by such physical torture. So they could not exploit him even with something as terrible as crucifixion. He still maintained his quality. Maybe someone can physically harm and kill a joyful person, but you cannot exploit him. Exploitation means he must be placed at a disadvantage, which cannot be done if you are truly joyful.

"Compassion means an all-encompassing passion."

Questioner: *Sometimes in our compassion when we reach out to people, their situation also takes a toll on us and we become unhappy. How do we keep ourselves from being affected?*

Sadhguru: If you are compassionate, you will never be affected. If you are kind, you will be affected. Kindness is an insult. Suppose you went to your friend's house. If he is not being loving to you, if he is just being very kind to you, will you feel great or will you feel insulted?

Participant: Insulted.

Sadhguru: That is what you are doing. If you are kind, it will affect you. If you are compassionate, it will not affect you. Compassion means you have a deep passion towards everything – whatever you see and whatever you are in touch with. When your passion becomes all-inclusive, that is compassion. When you are intensely involved with everything in the existence, that is compassion. Now it will not affect you. This is life. This is an intense way of being alive. If you are passionate with everything, you would be passionate with the sun coming up, you would be passionate with the snow falling, you would be passionate with the flowers blooming. When you are like this, would life affect you in a negative way? It will not.

When you are an unconscious existence, there is no way not to be affected. When your whole life is just a reaction to what you live in, how will you not be affected? This is like having a thorn bush in your garden, but you want to grow apples out of it. How can you grow apples out of a thorn bush? There is no such technology anywhere. If you want apples, you must plant an apple tree. That is what is needed.

Right now, who you are is everything that has come to you in bits and pieces from somebody else. How do you make these bits and pieces harmonious, joyful and complete? You can try as hard as you want, but you will never make it so. The sooner you realize this, the better. Most people take a lifetime to realize that. Once you realize it is not going to work, that is when you have to turn inward. If everything is going well in your life, that is when you should come to your senses. Most people come to their senses when things go dead wrong. You should not wait till that point. When things are going well, you must come to your senses.

The moment you carry the past and future, you become a donkey. Carrying that burden, there is no way anyone can be compassionate. They can only pretend. When you are so light that nothing matters, only then you can be truly compassionate. Love and compassion flow out of any person when there is no burden at all. What we normally carry as love, which is a great burden, is not really love. It is simply our own needs and greed covered up with a raiment of love. You can taste love and compassion in your life only when you are in this moment, fresh, absolutely without any burden. If you are carrying the burden of the past with you, there is no way it is possible. There may be some moments in your life when you felt true compassion towards something or somebody. At that moment, all your personality, who you are, what you are, everything would have melted. You were simply there, that moment. Only when you are like that, such compassion is possible.

In terms of emotion, compassion is the highest thing that a person can go through. Only somebody who lives in compassion is a real seeker. Compassion means an all-encompassing passion – your passion is no longer discriminatory. Whatever is in touch with you right now, you are deeply passionate with that. Whatever it is, if you look at something you are not just casually looking at anything; there is nothing casual in your life. Everything is with total passion. You breathe with passion, you walk with passion, you live with passion – your very existence is with absolute involvement with everything. This is compassion. This has got nothing to do with anybody. Even if nobody is here you can live in great compassion.

"Love is not a joy; it is a deep, wonderful pain."

Questioner: *If we carry the joy of love, can we walk the spiritual path with ease?*

Sadhguru: Love is not a joy; it is a deep, wonderful pain. It is a very deep, tearing, wonderful pain. Everything within you should tear – only then you know what love is. If you felt pleasant, that is not love – it is just convenience. Maybe you felt a little affection. But if you felt loving, everything inside you really tears apart. It is painful but wonderful.

When you are in love, everything that you do is love. If you eat, it will be love. Whether you work for that person or you do not do anything for the person and you just sit there, it will be love. But today, we have imbibed this idea, we have started using this term "love making." Only a certain act is supposed to be love. You cannot *make* love. If you allow it, it may happen to you. Love is never really exclusive. Love includes everything. When you are in love, you look at your dog, you will love it; you look at a tree, you love it; you look at a flower, you love it; you look at the sky, you will love it.

When you are in love, everything becomes beautiful. If only one person has become beautiful for you, there is no love in you. It is only lust wanting to express itself decently. Love is a quality, not an act. Meditation also is a quality, not an act. Spirituality is a quality, not an act. It is a new dimension. It is not something you do, it is something that you move into. It is something that you allow to overpower you. Otherwise there is no spirituality. If you think you are going to become spiritual, it is never going to happen. You become vulnerable, only then there is spirituality. If you stand like a rock, there is no spirituality.

〜◍◍〜

"Emotionally, when you break the barriers of who you are, you call it love. That is the yoga of love or yoga of devotion."

Questioner: *Sadhguru, is falling in love or being in love with a person the same as devotion?*

Sadhguru: A devotee is insanely passionate. When you truly love somebody, you will naturally be devoted. How can you not be devoted? If you are not devoted to the person whom you love, there is really no love – it is only a mutual benefit scheme. It is just a socially "picked up" word. Maybe you are also saying it because everybody is saying, "I love you."

Love is essentially devotion, but normally if we have to distinguish between the two, we can say love still has conditions attached to it. Whatever your expectations are, only if those things are fulfilled, your love affair will continue. Devotion is not like that. It is unconditional. That is the beauty of it. Love also genuinely becomes a fulfilling and life-nurturing process for any human being only if it is unconditional. The moment it becomes conditional, it becomes a transaction. Human transactions on the physical, emotional and intellectual level are being referred to as love. They are useful. "You fulfill my need, I will fulfill your need" – it is utilitarian. It is just that we would not like to see it that way because that makes people's lives ugly. They want to give a beautiful name to it, so they generally call it love.

When you go to the temple, church, mosque or some other such place, people call it devotion. But if you decipher and look at it, there is rarely any devotion. I wouldn't say no one is devoted – definitely some people are – but generally, once again it is a transaction. You do whatever God is supposed to be expecting you to do, and then God is supposed to do many other things for you. If you pray, what is your prayer? The basis of your prayer is fear and greed, please see. "Give me this, give me that and save me." This is also a kind of a transaction, a deal. But this is a very unfair deal, because generally what man offers to God and what he asks in return is a very unfair.

The English expression, "falling in love," is really appropriate and very beautiful. They always talked about falling in love. Nobody is ever talking about standing up in love or climbing in love or flying in love, because always when what you consider as "myself" falls, a deep experience of love can happen within you.

Love and devotion are not two different things, but still in our life, we generally separate them because one is supposed to be towards a higher purpose and another is supposed to fulfill the day-to-day needs. But I would say there is no need to separate these two. Love is devotion and devotion is just love. Without love, how can anybody be devout? You don't become a devotee just because you have subscribed to a certain religion, creed or whatever. A devotee cannot subscribe himself to anything – he is just drawn.

I should tell you an example.

Ramakrishna Paramahamsa lived as a very intense devotee most of his life. He was a mad devotee. There is no devotee who is not mad. If one is not mad, one is not a devotee because devotion is madness – a very beautiful madness, but it is madness. So, Ramakrishna was an ecstatic and insane man.

Now with a certain distance of time it is very easy to say, "He is Paramahamsa," but if you lived with him it would be very different. Suppose your neighbor jumps over into your garden in the middle of the night, comes and hugs your tree and starts screaming and crying, would you think he got enlightened or would you think he is drunk and crazy? This is what Ramakrishna was doing. He would burst into tears anywhere and cry like a baby. If he sees a tree, if he sees a cloud, if he sees the sun or the moon, he would cry like crazy. You would not think he was enlightened. You would definitely think he was insane.

Ramakrishna was a devotee of Kali. For him, Kali was not a deity – Kali was a living reality. She danced in front of him, ate from his own hands, came when he called, and left him dripping with ecstasy. This was real. It was actually happening. Chemically, he was all ecstasy. One day he was sitting on the banks of the Hoogli River, and a very great yogi, a rare yogi, Totapuri, came that way. Though Ramakrishna's body, mind and emotion were dripping with ecstasy, his being was longing to go beyond this ecstasy. Because somewhere there was an awareness that even this ecstasy is a bondage.

Still, the sweetness of ecstasy that he experienced was too much to leave and go. This is not any different from a drunkard being addicted to his drink or a drug addict being addicted to some substance. This should not be misunderstood. The only thing that is different is, alcohol and drugs will damage the system. This devoted ecstasy will not damage the system because this is internal. It is beautiful, there is no question about it. But the addiction, the attachment and the longing for that is the same and the limitation is also the same. Whenever Ramakrishna had contact with Kali – his object of devotion – he would be dripping with ecstasy, and he was fine with that. When Totapuri came, this transpired between them:

Totapuri said, "This is very simple. You have the necessary energy. You just have to empower your awareness. You are empowering your emotion, you are empowering your body, you are empowering the chemistry within you – you are not empowering your awareness."

Ramakrishna said, "Ok, I will empower my awareness and sit still."

But the moment he had a vision of Kali, he again went into uncontrollable states of love and ecstasy. Any number of times he sat down, but the moment he saw Kali he just flew off.

Then Totapuri said, "Next time Kali appears, you have to take a sword and cut her into pieces."

Ramakrishna asked, "Where do I get the sword from?"

Totapuri replied, "From the same place you get Kali from. If you are able to create a whole Kali, why can't you create a sword to cut her? You can do it. Get ready."

Again, the moment Kali came, he burst into ecstasy and forgot about the sword, the awareness and everything.

So then Totapuri told him, "Sit this time. The moment Kali comes... look at this," he picked up a piece of glass and said, "with this piece of glass, I'm going to cut you where you are stuck. When I cut that, you create the sword and cut Kali down."

So when Ramakrishna was just on the edge of ecstasy, when Kali appeared in his vision, Totapuri took a piece of glass and cut him really deep across his forehead. Then Ramakrishna created the sword and cut Kali down. He became free from the Mother and the ecstasy of feeding off her, and that is when he truly became a Paramahamsa. Till then he was a lover, he was a devotee, he was a child to the Mother Goddess that he created.

"When love reaches its peak, it naturally becomes reverence."

Questioner: *In the tradition, we were always taught to be reverential towards God or the highest aspect. So how to reconcile this with Mirabai or Akka Mahadevi who took God as their lover?*

Sadhguru: Where there is no love, how can reverence come? When love reaches its peak, it naturally becomes reverence. People who are talking about reverence without love know neither this nor that. All they know is fear. So probably you are referring to God-fearing people. These sages and saints, especially the seers like Akka Mahadevi, Mirabai or Anusuya and so many of them in the past, have taken to this form of worship because it was more suitable for them – they could emote much more easily than they could intellectualize things. They just used their emotions to reach their Ultimate nature. Using emotion and reaching the Ultimate nature is what is called bhakti yoga.

In every culture, there are different forms of worship. Some people worship God as the master and themselves as the slaves. Sometimes they even take God as their servant or as a partner in everything that they do. Yet others worship him as a friend, as a lover, or as their own child like Balakrishna. Generally, you become the feminine and you hold him as the ultimate *purusha* – masculine. How you worship is not at all the point; the whole point is just how deeply you relate.

These are the different attitudes, but whatever the attitude, the love affair is such that you are not expecting anything from the other side. Not even a response. You crave for it. But if there is no response, you are not going to be angry, you are not going to be disappointed – nothing. Your life is just to crave and make something else tremendously more important than yourself. That is the fundamental thing.

In the whole path of bhakti, the important thing is just this, that something else is far more important than you. So Akka, Mirabai and others like them, their bhakti was in that form and they took this mode of worship where they worshipped God – whether Shiva or Krishna – as their husband. In India, when a woman comes to a certain age, marriage is almost like a must, and it anyway happens. They wanted to eliminate that dimension of being married once again to another man, so they chose the Lord himself as their husband so that they don't need any other relationship in their lives.

How a devotee relates to his object of devotion does not really matter because the purpose of the path of devotion is just dissolution. The only objective of a devotee is to dissolve into his object of devotion. Whichever way they could relate best, that is how they would do it. The reason why you asked this question in terms of reverence juxtaposed with being a lover or a husband is because the word "love" or "being a lover" is always understood as a physical aspect. That is why this question has come. How can you be physical with somebody and still be reverential? This has been the tragedy of humanity that lovers have not known how to be reverential to each other. In fact the very objective of love is to dissolve into someone else.

If you look at love as an emotion, you can see that love is a vehicle to bring oneness. It is the longing to become one with the other which we are referring to as love. When it is taken to its peak, it is very natural to become reverential towards what you consider worthwhile being "one" with. For whatever sake, you are willing to dissolve yourself. It is natural to be reverential towards that. Otherwise how would you feel that it is worthwhile to dissolve into? If you think it is something you can use or something you can just relate to and be benefited by, there can be no love. Always, the object of love is to dissolve. So, whatever you consider is worthwhile to dissolve your own self into, you are bound to be reverential towards that; there is no other way to be.

"Devotion by practice usually does not take you anywhere."

Questioner: *How do you become a devotee?*

Sadhguru: Today, because of the way we have cultivated the intellect and our education systems, our social order demands a certain level of intellect. All of the physical sciences have grown out of intellect, doubts, questioning and experimenting. If a mind like that tries to be devout, it can only lead to deception.

Most of the people who believe they are devout are only deceiving themselves, because a thinking, questioning mind cannot really become a devotee. Not that there is no element of devotion at all, but such a person cannot become a true devotee, because a devotee is only seeing how to dissolve with his object of devotion. He has no agenda of his own. Whatever the object of devotion dictates, he goes that way. A devotee is never thinking in terms of his wellbeing. An intellect cannot do that. So, trying to put the intellect under the carpet and walk away is not going to happen because it will obviously pop up somewhere else and bother you.

Cultivated devotion is just deception. When you are overwhelmed by something, you will naturally be devoted to it. Devotion by practice usually does not take you anywhere. If you try to practice devotion, it will lead you into so many kinds of hallucinations, that you start believing all kinds of things. If you are overwhelmed by something or someone, naturally you become devout. A devotee means not much of him is left. A devotee means, even his physical body will change to resemble his object of devotion. Everything in you becomes like the object of your devotion.

A wonderful example of this was this incredible man in Tamil Nadu.

There was a seeress, a lady saint in India, whose name was Mayamma. Mayamma means "the illusory mother." When I say she was a saint, don't think she was certified by someone. These are sages; they are not stamped by someone. Their very life is a stamp. No one knows where this woman came from. She was a really puny woman, less than five feet tall. Looking at her facial features I think she came from Nepal, but definitely she was not from southern India because she did not even know the language, and she never bothered to learn the language. She just walked on the streets in the southernmost tip of India which is known as Kanyakumari. If somebody gave her something to eat, she ate; otherwise she just walked around.

She came as a young woman and people wondered who she was and thought she was crazy. She would be dancing and singing and crying on the streets. Then somehow she drew dogs, which gathered around her. Always, eight or ten dogs would follow her wherever she went. They did not gather for her saintly qualities; they gathered because she always fed them. She loved these dogs so much that she would steal for them. This bunch of dogs would follow her, and she would go to a restaurant where they would have a display of food. She would stand there and when no one was looking, she would grab all the food and throw it on the street. All the dogs would help themselves, and so naturally she was their friend. Many times she was thrashed by the restaurant owners. If she came anywhere near, everyone would take a stick, abuse her and send her off. But on one occasion, people saw her just sitting on the water and floating around. She would simply sit on the water and float all over the place on the ocean. When she wanted to come back she would swim, otherwise she would just float upon the water and go away into the ocean.

Once people saw this, they stopped abusing her and beating her because she was better than those who walk. Some people started worshipping her, and some people gathered around her, but she never spoke – not a word. She walked and some people walked behind her. If she sat, they sat around her. The dogs also sat, the people also sat. But she never said a word or gave any teaching.

Then, as she was aging, a famous musician wanted to build a small house for her. He moved her from that place and put her up in the town of Salem which is away from the ocean. She loved the ocean so much. They should have built something for her by the ocean, but for some reason they built it in Salem, and a few people gathered around her and were devoted to her. She left her body there.

There is a mountain very close to this place with a hill station. I was staying at this hill station when someone told me about this saint. They told me, "Mayamma's place is here," and they showed me her picture. The moment I saw the picture I said, "I want to go there," and drove down. It happened to be a full moon day and there was a small Samadhi – a small grave – that had been built for her. The place is reverberating like crazy. This is a fantastic place.

The people there said, "Today is Purnima, the full moon day. Stay back, we are having some *prasad*." They were serving everyone dinner. The best thing was that there was this one little man who was devoted to Mayamma. Mayamma lived outdoors her whole life, so her face was all weather-beaten. She was like a Nepali so the features were mildly mongoloid. This man was a southern Indian man. He had been so devoted to her. When he came in front of me, I saw his face had become exactly like hers. This is a devotee of the highest order. It was so amazing seeing him.

Devotion is that kind of thing. If you dismantle the structures of who you are and get completely absorbed into something, if that something is powerful enough, it will just imprint upon you. That is the idea of devotion. You are not acting it out; you can become that. It is not about being devoted to somebody or something; it is just that it is the highest level of perception. You can imprint yourself with what you are seeking because you opened yourself up completely.

Sadhguru

Yogi, mystic and visionary, Sadhguru is a spiritual master with a difference. Absolute clarity of perception places him in a unique space, not only in matters spiritual but in business, environmental and international affairs, and opens a new door on all that he touches.

Probing and passionate, insightful, logical and unfailingly witty, Sadhguru's talks have earned him the reputation of a speaker and opinion-maker of international renown. He has been conferred the Padma Vibhushan by the Government of India in 2017, the highest annual civilian award, accorded for exceptional and distinguished service. He has been a lead speaker at the United Nations General Assembly, a regular at the World Economic Forum, and a special invitee at the Australian Leadership Retreat, Indian Economic Summit, and TED. His astute and incisive grasp of world affairs, as well as his unerringly scientific approach to human wellbeing have had a transformative influence at establishments such as the World Bank, House of Lords (UK), the World Presidents' Organization, Massachusetts Institute of Technology (MIT), the University of Oxford, Harvard University, Stanford University, Duke University, IMD Business School, the London Business School, Google, and Microsoft, to name a few.

With a celebratory engagement with life on all levels, Sadhguru's areas of active involvement encompass fields as diverse as architecture and visual design, poetry and painting, aviation and driving, ecology and horticulture, sports and music. Sadhguru has initiated Rally for Rivers, a nationwide campaign to revitalize India's severely depleted rivers, which has found phenomenal support among India's people and leadership. He is the designer of several unique buildings and consecrated spaces at the Isha Yoga Center, which have received wide attention for their combination of intense sacred power with strikingly innovative eco-friendly aesthetics.

app.sadhguru.org

isha.sadhguru.org

facebook.com/sadhguru

twitter.com/SadhguruJV

youtube.com/sadhguru

rallyforrivers.org

Isha Foundation

Isha Foundation is a non-profit human-service organization, supported by over nine million volunteers in over 250 centers worldwide. Recognizing the possibility of each person to empower another, Isha Foundation has created a massive movement that is dedicated to address all aspects of human wellbeing, without subscribing to any particular ideology, religion or race.

Isha is involved in several path-breaking outreach initiatives: Action for Rural Rejuvenation (ARR) enhances the quality of rural life through healthcare and disease prevention, community revitalization, women empowerment, the creation of sustainable livelihoods, and yoga programs. Isha Vidhya empowers rural children with quality education. Project GreenHands (PGH) initiates mass tree planting and creates a culture of care for the environment to keep this planet liveable for future generations.

Isha's unique approach in cultivating human potential has gained worldwide recognition and reflects in Isha Foundation's special consultative status with the Economic and Social Council (ECOSOC) of the United Nations.

The Foundation is headquartered at the Isha Yoga Center, at the base of the Velliangiri Mountains in southern India, and at the Isha Institute of Inner-sciences on the spectacular Cumberland Plateau in central Tennessee, USA.

isha.sadhguru.org

ishaoutreach.org

facebook.com/ishafoundation

twitter.com/ishafoundation

youtube.com/ishafoundation

Inner Engineering

Inner Engineering is offered as an intensive program for personal growth. The program and its environment establish the possibility to explore the higher dimensions of life and offers tools to re-engineer one's self through the inner science of yoga. Once given the tools to rejuvenate, people can optimize all aspects of health, inner growth and success. For those seeking professional and personal excellence, this program offers keys for meaningful and fulfilling relationships at work, home, community, and most importantly, within one's self.

Inner Engineering can be thought of as a synthesis of holistic sciences to help participants establish an inner foundation and vision for all dimensions of life and find the necessary balance between the challenges of a hectic career and the inner longing for peace and wellbeing.

The approach is a modern antidote to stress, and presents simple but powerful processes from yogic science to purify the system and increase health and inner wellbeing. Program components include guided meditations and transmission of the sacred Shambhavi Mahamudra. When practiced on a regular basis, these tools have the potential to enhance one's experience of life on many levels.

isha.sadhguru.org/IEO

Isha Yoga Center

Isha Yoga Center, founded under the aegis of Isha Foundation, is located at the foothills of the Velliangiri Mountains. Created as a powerful *sthana* (a center for inner growth), this popular destination attracts people from all parts of the world. It is unique in its offering of all aspects of yoga – gnana (knowledge), karma (action), kriya (energy), and bhakti (devotion) and revives the Guru-shishya paramparya (the traditional method of knowledge transfer from Master to disciple).

Isha Yoga Center provides a supportive environment for people to shift to healthier lifestyles, improve interpersonal relationships, seek a higher level of self-fulfillment, and realize their full potential.

The Center is located 30 km west of Coimbatore, a major industrial city in southern India which is well connected by air, rail, and road. All major national airlines operate regular flights into Coimbatore from Chennai, Delhi, Mumbai, and

Bengaluru. Train services are available from all major cities in India. Regular bus and taxi services are also available from Coimbatore to the Center.

Visitors are advised to contact the Center for availability and reservation of accommodation well in advance, as it is generally heavily booked.

isha.sadhguru.org/IYC

Sadhguru

Isha Yoga Center (map)

Dhyanalinga

The Dhyanalinga is a powerful and unique energy form created
by Sadhguru from the essence of yogic sciences. Situated at the
Isha Yoga Center, it is the first of its kind to be completed in
over 2000 years. The Dhyanalinga is a meditative space that
does not subscribe to any particular faith or belief system nor
does it require any ritual, prayer, or worship.

The Dhyanalinga was consecrated by Sadhguru after three
years of an intense process of prana pratishtha. Housed within
an architecturally striking pillarless dome structure, the
Dhyanalinga's energies allow even those unaware of meditation
to experience a deep state of meditativeness, revealing the
essential nature of life.

A special feature of the Dhyanalinga complex are the
Theerthakunds, consecrated subterranean water bodies,
energized by rasalingas. A dip in these vibrant pools significantly
enhances one's spiritual receptivity and is a good preparation

to receive the Grace of the Dhyanalinga. The waters of the Theerthakunds also rejuvenate the body, and bring health and wellbeing.

The Dhyanalinga draws many thousands of people every week, who converge to experience a deep sense of inner peace.

dhyanalinga.org

Adiyogi – the Source of Yoga

Over 15,000 years ago, predating all religion, Adiyogi, the first yogi, transmitted the science of yoga to his seven disciples, the Saptarishis. He expounded 112 ways through which human beings can transcend their limitations and reach their ultimate potential. Adiyogi's offerings are tools for individual transformation, as individual transformation is the only way to transform the world. His fundamental message is that "in is the only way out" for human wellbeing and liberation.

On the auspicious night of Mahashivaratri at Isha Yoga Center, an iconic face of "Adiyogi – the Source of Yoga" was unveiled by the Hon'ble Prime Minister Narendra Modi. A towering 112 feet high, this glorious face represents the 112 ways one can attain to one's ultimate nature. Installed near the Adiyogi is the Yogeshwar Linga, which was consecrated by Sadhguru, as manifestation of five of the major chakras in the

human system. Adiyogi, with the presence of the Yogeshwar Linga, has become a living entity.

To create a joyful and peaceful world, humanity must know that true wellbeing can only be found within, and they must be inspired and empowered with the necessary tools to turn inward. The tools for transformation that Adiyogi offered to humanity thousands of years ago are not only relevant but essential today. The 112-ft face of Adiyogi is a powerful reminder and inspiration to all.

isha.sadhguru.org/adiyogi

Worldwide Centers

INDIA

Isha Yoga Center
Velliangiri Foothills,
IshanaVihar Post,
Coimbatore 641114 India.
Telephone: +91 83000 83111
Email: info@ishafoundation.org

USA

Isha Institute of Inner-sciences
951 Isha Lane, McMinnville,
TN 37110 USA.
Telephone: +1-931-668-1900
Email: usa@ishafoundation.org

UK

Isha Foundation

1 Silex Street , London SE1 0DW

Telephone: +44-79 56 99 87 29

Email: uk@ishafoundation.org

OTHER CENTERS

(For contact info, visit ishafoundation.org/ContactUs)

ASIA-PACIFIC

Australia
China
Hong Kong
Indonesia
Malaysia
Nepal
New Zealand
Singapore

AFRICA

Kenya
South Africa
Uganda

EUROPE

France
Germany
Netherlands
Sweden
Switzerland

MIDDLE EAST

Lebanon
Oman
Qatar
United Arab Emirates

Isha Kriya

Isha Kriya™ is a simple yet potent practice rooted in the timeless wisdom of the yogic sciences. "Isha" refers to that which is the source of creation; "kriya" literally means "internal action." The purpose of Isha Kriya is to help an individual get in touch with the source of his existence, to create life according to his own wish and vision.

Through Isha Kriya, a 12-minute practice, an individual can pursue immediate and ultimate wellbeing, experiencing success in the social sphere, while nourishing the inner longing for the deeper dimensions of life. Isha Kriya empowers an individual towards a stress-free way of being, and promotes enhanced clarity, heightened energy levels, and a state of peacefulness and joy. Daily practice of Isha Kriya brings health, dynamism and happiness. It is a powerful tool to cope with the hectic pace of modern life.

Isha Kriya requires no special physical agility or previous

experience of yoga to practice. It integrates seamlessly into one's daily life, bringing the possibilities of a spiritual process – which were once available only to yogis and ascetics – to every human being in the comfort of their own home. Created by Sadhguru, it has the potential to transform the life of anyone who is willing to invest just a few minutes a day. The instructions for Isha Kriya are given below.

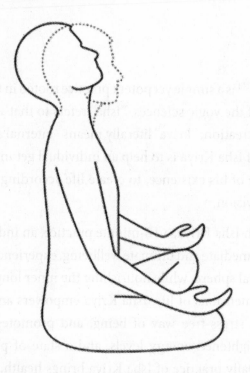

PREPARATION

- Sit facing east in a cross-legged posture, with your spine comfortably erect.

- Keep your hands upon your thighs, with your palms facing up.

- With your face slightly upturned, eyes closed, keep a mild focus between your eyebrows.

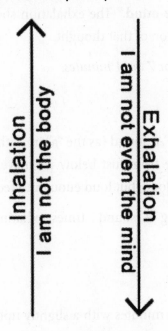

The breathing should be as shown in this diagram

THE MEDITATION

This meditation happens in three stages:

Stage 1

- Inhale and exhale gently, slowly.

- With each inhalation, mentally say to yourself: **"I am not the body."** The inhalation should last the whole duration of that thought.

- With each exhalation, mentally say to yourself: **"I am not even the mind."** The exhalation should last for the whole duration of that thought.

- *Repeat this for 7 to 11 minutes.*

Stage 2

- Utter a long "A" sound (as the "a" in "father"). The sound should come from just below the navel. You need not utter it very loud, but loud enough to feel the vibration.

- Utter the long "A" sound 7 times, exhaling fully into each sound.

Stage 3

- Sit for 5 to 6 minutes with a slightly upturned face, and keep a mild focus between your eyebrows.

- *The total time of this practice is between 12 to 18 min. You can sit longer if you want.*

Please Note:

- While you sit for the Isha Kriya, do not pay attention to the activity of the mind or body. Whatever is happening in your body or your mind, just ignore it and simply sit there.

- Do not take a break in between, as it will disturb the reorganization of energies that happens during the practice.

- Each time you do the *kriya*, you must do it for a minimum of 12 minutes, and twice a day for 48 days (considered as a full *mandala* or cycle), or once a day for 90 days. This is your commitment. This is your *Gurudakshina* (a traditional offering to a Guru or Spiritual Master).

- Anyone can practice this kriya and enjoy its benefits. Simply follow the instructions without making any changes. This is a simple but very potent kriya.

- You can remind yourself that "I am not the body. I am not even the mind" anytime during the day.

Questioner: *What can I possibly gain out of this?*

Sadhguru: Where is the need to meditate, first of all? Starting the process of life was not your conscious choice, it "happened" to you. When you were born your body was so small, and now it has grown. So obviously, the body is something that you gathered. It is an accumulation. What you call as "my body" is an accumulation of food. Similarly, what you call as "my mind" is an accumulation of impressions.

Whatever you accumulate can be yours, but it can never be you. The very fact you accumulated it means that you gathered it from somewhere else. Today you could gather a 70 kg body, but you can decide to make it a 60 kg body. You don't go looking for those 10 kg, because they were an accumulation. Once you drop it, it is gone. Similarly, with your mind, it is an accumulation of impressions.

The moment you are identified in your experience, the moment you are identified with something that you are not, your perception goes completely haywire. You cannot perceive life the way it is; your perception is hugely distorted. So the moment you start experiencing this body, which you gathered from outside, as "myself," the moment you start experiencing the impressions that you have in your mind as "myself," you cannot perceive life the way it is. You will only perceive life the way it is necessary for your survival, and not the way it really is.

Yet once you have come as a human being, survival is very important, but it is not enough. If you had come here like any other creature on this planet, stomach full – life would be settled. But once you come here as a human being, life does not end with survival. Actually, for a human being, life begins only after survival is fulfilled.

So meditation gives you an experience, an inner state where what is you and what is yours is separated. There is a little distance, there is a little space between what is you and what you have accumulated. For now we can understand this as meditation.

What is the use of doing this? It brings an absolute clarity of perception. You see life just the way it is. No distortions about it; simply seeing life just the way it is. Right now if we see the very room we are in as a world, your ability to go through this world is only to the extent that you clearly see it. If I have no clarity of vision but if I have confidence and if I try to go through this, I'm going to be a bumbling idiot. Whenever there is no perception, people try to overcome that by building confidence in them. Without the clarity of perception people are trying to make it up with other kinds of substitutes; there is no substitute for clarity.

Once you understand this you naturally become meditative; you want to clear up everything and just look at life the way it is, because you want to walk through life with least amount of friction, without stumbling on this or that.

Questioner: *Why should my head be slightly upturned?*

Sadhguru: Sitting with your head slightly upturned is not because you want to see something floating in the sky or imagine something. You keep your head upturned because when your system "looks" upward it becomes receptive. It is like opening a window. This is about becoming receptive to Grace. When you become willing and receptive, your body naturally arches up.

Questioner: *What does this meditation do?*

Sadhguru: This Kriya will create a certain space between you and your body, between you and your mind. If at all there is any struggle in your life, it is because you identify yourself with these limited aspects of yourself.

So the essence of meditation is that it creates a space, a distance between you and what you refer to as your "mind." All the suffering you go through is manufactured in your mind, isn't it so? If you distance yourself from the mind, can there be suffering in you? This is the end of suffering.

Now while you are meditating, there is a distance between you and your mind, and you do feel peaceful. The problem is that the moment you open your eyes, you are again stuck with your mind.

If you meditate every day, a day will come when you open your eyes, and you can still experience that the mind is there and you are here. This is the end of suffering. When you are no longer identified with your body and mind, you will be in touch with the source of Creation within you. Once this happens, Grace happens.

Whether you are here, or beyond, this is the end of suffering. That means your whole karmic bag – your past, or your unconscious mind – has been kept aside. It cannot have any influence over you. Once the past has no influence over you, then life becomes a huge potential. Every breath becomes such a tremendous possibility in your life, because the past is not playing any role in your existence here now. If you sit here, you are absolute life. Life becomes effortless.

Questioner: *What is the importance of the breath? Is there more to breathing well than being healthy?*

Sadhguru: Breath is the thread which ties you to the body. If I take away your breath, your body will fall apart. It is the breath that has tied you to the body. What you call as your body and what you call as "me" have been tied together with breath. And this breath decides many aspects of who you are right now. For different levels of thought and emotion that you go through, your breath takes on different types of patterns. If you are angry you will be breathing one way. You are peaceful, you breathe another way. You are happy, you breathe another way. You are sad, you will breathe another way. Have you noticed this?

Based on this conversely is the science of pranayama and kriya: by consciously breathing in a particular way, the very way you think, feel, understand and experience life can be changed.

This breath can be used in so many ways as a tool to do other things with the body and the mind. You will see with the Isha Kriya, we are using a simple process of breath, but the kriya itself is not in the breath. Breath is just a tool. Breath is an induction, but what happens is not about the breath.

Whichever way you breathe, that is the way you think. Whichever way you think, that is the way you breathe. Your whole life, your whole unconscious mind is written into your breath. If you just read your breath, your past, present and future is written there, in the way you breathe.

Once you realize this, life becomes very different. It needs to be known experientially; it is not something you can propound like this. If you know the bliss of simply sitting here, the blissfulness of just being able to simply sit here, not think anything, not do anything, simply sit here, just being life, then life would be very different.

In a way, what this means is today there is scientific proof that without taking a drop of alcohol, without taking any substance you can simply sit here and get drugged or stoned or drunk by yourself. If you are aware in a certain way, you can activate the system in such a way that if you sit here it is an enormous pleasure. Once simply sitting and breathing is such a great pleasure, you will become very genial, flexible, wonderful because all the time you are in a great state within yourself. No hangover. Mind becomes sharper than ever before.

Questioner: *What effect does uttering the sound "Aaa" have on me?*

Sadhguru: When you utter the sound "Aaa," the maintenance center in your body gets activated. This is *Manipuraka chakra*, or the navel center. Manipuraka is just three-fourths of an inch below your navel. When you were in your mother's womb, the "maintenance" pipe was connected there. Now the tube is gone, but the maintenance center is still in your navel.

Now as there is a physical body, there is a whole energy body that we generally refer to as either prana or *shakti*. This energy, or prana, flows through the body in certain established patterns; it is not moving randomly. There are 72,000 different ways in which it moves. In other words, there are 72,000 pathways in the system through which it is flowing. So *nadis* are pathways or channels in the system. They do not have a physical manifestation; if you cut the body and look inside, you will not find these nadis. But as you become more and more aware, you will notice the energy is not moving at random, it is moving in established pathways.

When you utter the sound "Aaa," you will see the reverberation will start about three-fourths of an inch below the navel and spread right across the body. Sound "Aaa" is the only reverberation which spreads right across the body because this is the only place where the 72,000 nadis meet and redistribute themselves. They all meet at Manipuraka and redistribute themselves. This is the only point in the body like that. If you utter the sound "Aaa," the reverberations of this sound are carried right across the system.

This reverberation can assist greatly in energizing your maintenance center. Activating this center will bring health, dynamism, prosperity and wellbeing.

Visit ishakriya.com and go through the Isha Kriya guided practice by Sadhguru.